Psychological Testing

A manager's guide

Fourth edition

John Toplis, a chartered occupational psychologist and a chartered member of the Chartered Institute of Personnel and Development, is a director of Prime Executive (a division of Charity People), a recruitment consultancy specialising in senior appointments in charitable and not-for-profit organisations, where he is additionally Head of Assessment and Development. He also works as an independent consultant.

John first worked as a psychologist at the National Institute of Industrial Psychology, where he was Head of Diagnostic Studies between 1963 and 1973. Between 1973 and 1984 he was Director of the Occupational Psychology Unit at Barking College of Technology, where he introduced testing for careers guidance in local schools and advised local industry on the use of psychometrics in assessment centres for senior appointments.

Between 1984 and 1999 John held a number of senior appointments in the Post Office/Royal Mail, including Head of Psychological Services (1984–91), when he was responsible for all the selection methods in the Post Office businesses. Between 1991 and 1994 he managed major programmes of assessment across the Post Office businesses involving over 1,000 top managers.

John is a past chair of the Occupational Psychology section of the British Psychological Society, and was Secretary/Treasurer of the International Test Commission for ten years.

Professor Victor Dulewicz has worked at Henley Management College since 1986 and is currently Head of the Human Resource Management and Organisational Behaviour Faculty, and Director of Assessment Services. He lectures on personality, team roles, emotional intelligence and management assessment and development on most courses, and acts as a syndicate and individual adviser on executive programmes. He led a major government-funded project investigating competences for boards of directors and is currently researching board and company performance, and leadership. He was also a Governor of the College from 1998 to 2003.

In the past, he worked as an occupational psychologist for Rank Xerox and the Civil Service Selection Board, and was for nine years Manager of Assessment and Occupational Psychology for the STC Group (now Nortel).

Since 1986 he has advised many large blue-chip companies on management assessment and development, specifically on competences, psychological testing, emotional intelligence and assessment centres. He has written over 100 articles and presented at numerous national and international conferences on these subjects. He was a section editor of the handbook *Assessment and Selection in Organisations* (Wiley, 1989), co-author of *Good Practice for Directors: Standards for the board* (IoD, 1995) and co-author of *Making Sense of Emotional Intelligence* (NFER-Nelson, 2002). Further details of his current work and recent publications can be found on www.dulewicz.com.

Victor Dulewicz is a chartered occupational psychologist, a Fellow of both the British Psychological Society and the Chartered Institute of Personnel and Development, and a member of the Institute of Directors.

Professor Clive Fletcher is the Managing Director of Personnel Assessment Ltd. He was formerly Professor of Occupational Psychology at Goldsmiths' College, University of London, where he still holds the title of Emeritus Professor after leaving to work in private practice. He is also Visiting Professor at Henley Management College. Clive is a chartered occupational psychologist and one of the relatively few psychologists to be elected to Fellowship of the British Psychological Society (BPS). He is formerly chair of the Occupational Psychology section of the BPS. Clive has published nearly 200 books, chapters, journal articles and conference papers on psychological assessment in work settings. He is author of the standard CIPD text on performance appraisal and Director of the Psychology of Managing Performance course, an element of the CIPD's Psychology of Management programme. Clive has acted in an advisory and consultancy capacity to many private sector organisations and to government departments – he is currently independent adviser to the Cabinet Office. His knowledge and experience in the assessment field is recognised internationally. He has given invited papers at conferences in the USA and throughout Europe. He is a member of the Scientific Advisory Board of Behavioral Sciences Research Press, based in Dallas, and a member of the Professional Advisory Board of Career Harmony Inc. Further details of his publications can be found on www.personnel-assessment.com.

The Chartered Institute of Personnel and Development is the leading publisher of books and reports for personnel and training professionals, students, and all those concerned with the effective management and development of people at work. For details of all our titles, please contact the publishing department:

tel: 020-8263 3387
fax: 020-8263 3850
e-mail publish@cipd.co.uk

The catalogue of all CIPD titles can be viewed on the CIPD website:
www.cipd.co.uk/bookstore

Psychological Testing

A manager's guide

Fourth edition

John Toplis
Victor Dulewicz
Clive Fletcher

Chartered Institute of Personnel and Development

Published by the Chartered Institute of Personnel and Development,
CIPD House, Camp Road, London, SW19 4UX

First edition published 1987
Second edition published 1991
Third edition published 1997
This edition published 2005

Design by Beacon GDT, Mitcheldean, Gloucestershire
Typeset by Fakenham Photosetting
Printed in Great Britain by The Cromwell Press, Trowbridge, Wiltshire

British Library Cataloguing in Publication Data
A catalogue of this publication is available from the British Library

ISBN 0 85292 968 4

Chartered Institute of Personnel and Development, CIPD House,
Camp Road, London, SW19 4UX
Tel: 020 8971 9000   Fax: 020 8263 3333
Email: cipd@cipd.co.uk   Website: www.cipd.co.uk
Incorporated by Royal Charter.   Registered Charity No. 1079797

Contents

Preface to the Fourth Edition

In writing this Fourth Edition we continue to have four aims:

- to alert readers to the benefits of 'good' testing
- to warn of the disadvantages and dangers of 'bad' testing
- to give a 'balanced view' of the merits and disadvantages of testing, illustrating points by means of case studies and frequently asked questions
- to let readers decide whether to use tests (or continue testing) in the future.

This preface addresses five issues:

- the audiences that we had in mind when writing the book
- the general changes in the world of testing since the first edition of this book was published in 1987
- our views on the current 'state of play'
- our views on the benefits and on areas of concern
- how the new edition is structured, with a summary of the differences between the Fourth and Third Editions.

AUDIENCES

The full title of this book, *Psychological Testing: A manager's guide,* indicates the main audience for whom the book is written. It is about tests that are normally used in the world of work or in activities that are associated with employment. Our focus is on the area of selection but there is mention of issues such as career choice or planning for a change of career, or even planning for retirement. The book does not aim to cover the many tests that have been designed for use in the areas of clinical or educational psychology.

There are several reasons why the book has been written mainly for managers. One is that managers normally decide on testing policy in an organisation – whether tests should be used and in what circumstances – and we believe that this book can help them make those decisions. Next there are the issues of what tests to use and how to use them. Again, we believe that the book will be helpful. The tests and test publishers referenced here are representative of leading professional standards, but we have strongly resisted the selection of some tests as 'best buys' – to be effective, tests have to be:

- well designed, with a specific group or groups in mind
- used in appropriate circumstances, and
- used by people who are thoroughly trained in their use – asking for a recommendation on the 'best test' is analogous to asking about the 'best medicine' or the 'best car'.

We believe that the book may also be of interest to a number of other groups. For example, there are those studying to be managers, whether in the human resource or personnel specialism, or in other functions. We have also considered the needs of those who are about to take tests for the first time and who are wondering what they might do by way of preparation (see Appendix III).

CHANGES IN THE WORLD OF TESTING SINCE 1987

The First Edition was published at a time when aptitude and reasoning tests were widely used in the UK as a way of selecting for practical and clerical work. Tests also featured as part of many recruitment programmes for the selection of graduates. In contrast, relatively little use was made of personality questionnaires – although versions of the 16PF, a personality questionnaire, had been available for some time, the first edition of the Occupational Personality Questionnaire (OPQ) was published in 1982. At this time, the British Psychological Society approved each of the relevant training courses, considering both the design of the tests and the qualifications and experience of the trainers. Many of those trained in testing were managers who wanted to be able to use tests in their own organisation without involving the psychologists who had taken part in the design or distribution of the tests.

By the time that the Second Edition was published in 1991 there had been a number of important changes. For a number of reasons the British Psychological Society decided that it would not continue to approve every training course, and instead worked on the development of certificates of competence in psychological testing. The Level A certificate – dealing with reasoning and aptitude tests – had just been made available. Those attaining this certificate were regarded as being able to decide which of these tests might be used in particular circumstances.

There were a number of other changes. One was the rapid growth in the use of personality questionnaires. Although some were well designed and were made available only to those who had attended training courses supervised by chartered psychologists, others lacked the supporting data normally associated with well-researched instruments, and were said to require little or no training in their use. Second, tests became the subject of marketing and advertising, some companies employing sales staff paid on a commission basis. Third, large numbers of 'consultants' began offering advice on the uses of tests; some were fully qualified occupational psychologists or non-psychologists who had attended lengthy training courses of the kind run at Birkbeck College or Goldsmiths' College (University of London), but others had only attended the short training courses originally designed so that people could use tests in their own organisations without the direct involvement of a psychologist.

When the Third Edition was published in 1997 we reported that the British Psychological Society had continued to work on the certificates of competence in psychological testing. So far as Level A was concerned, a distance-learning package had been published and was reviewed. Plans for a certificate of competency at Level B (personality testing) were well advanced. The British Psychological Society had started to produce reviews of ability and aptitude tests (Level A) and personality assessment instruments (Level B). So far as the use of tests is concerned, they have often featured as part of the assessment of staff during major reorganisation pro-grammes. For example, over 10,000 managers were tested when Royal Mail reorgan-ised in 1991, the tests and other assessment methods used varying with the grade of manager.

The certificates of competence in testing and the wider use of tests in reorganisation and other programmes did not mean that there had been universal improvement in the standards of use or interpretation of tests. Some tests continued to be sold with little or no evidence of their technical worth, and it should be remembered that test-ing can do harm to both organisations and to individuals if the wrong people are selec-ted or if there is unfair discrimination. In addition, some 'consultants' were continuing to offer advice on testing on the basis of little or no training, while efforts to market tests were ranging from 'free trials' to glossy newsletters and other publications.

THE CURRENT STATE OF PLAY

Our view at the time of writing is that the use of tests has continued to grow. In our experience most managers have now experienced tests or questionnaires of some kind, although this might be often as part of a team-building or other event rather than as part of a selection procedure. Related to this, the number of people qualified to use tests has continued to grow as more people obtain certificates of competence at Level A and Level B. Since 1991 a total of 17,495 people have obtained the Level A certificate, and since 1996 a total of 4,606 have obtained the Level B intermediate certificate (see Chapter 5). The British Psychological Society has set up a Psychological Testing Centre which supplies information about testing in general, how to obtain the certificates of competence, and reviews of individual tests.

Perhaps the greatest change has been in the availability of tests over the Internet. This means that people can be tested anywhere in the world, and some employers are attracted to the idea of screening applicants in this way. However, there is a whole series of issues to consider. One is that employers may consider only applicants with the highest test scores although those with more modest abilities may be better suited. Then there is a real danger of fraud by means of impersonation unless the identity of those being tested is carefully checked. There is also the risk of various forms of cheating, and issues about giving 'feedback' to those tested and the security of the data collected – what is seen as good practice in the UK and the guidelines and legislation that affect our work here does not apply worldwide.

Another change has been the speed with which organisations change. Whereas our parents may have joined a large commercial organisation and stayed with them for their working lives, our children are entering a world of work which is changing rapidly. In particular they are more likely to develop their careers by changing organisations rather than by simply changing jobs. This is making it harder to carry out long-term follow-up studies of the effectiveness of tests and other selection methods.

Testing is finding its way into new areas, particularly areas associated with higher education. For example, admission tests have been introduced for law and for medical students, and draft recommendations about 'fair admissions to higher education' are encouraging this trend. These and other developments associated with further and higher education are detailed in Chapter 12.

BENEFITS AND AREAS OF CONCERN

The potential benefits of testing have not changed since 1987. Better selection means that people are more productive and better able to meet their employer's needs in other ways. For example, studies have shown that better workers are at least three times more productive than others. More productive workers generally earn more and enjoy their work more than those who are struggling to keep up.

However, when writing the preface to the Second Edition we identified five areas of concern:

- test administration
- purchasing channels
- test quality
- graphology and other selection methods
- statistical inaccuracy.

These areas of concern remain and we hope that they will be of interest to readers.

Test administration

Our concern arises from the increased use of computers to administer, score and interpret the test results. It is easy to be impressed by the administration of tests over the Internet, the amount of text generated about a candidate by an 'expert system' and by the speed of production of the report. But basic questions must still be asked, including 'Are we confident that we really know the identity of the person who took this test?', 'Was the test appropriate for this vacancy?', 'Has appropriate training been given to those who will be using the results?', and 'Has the report produced by the expert system given a fair picture of the candidate?'

Purchasing channels

Tests are increasingly sold by sales staff rather than by psychologists. Such staff are sometimes recruited with the promise of high earnings from commission earned on sales made; they are not subject to any professional code of conduct, and may be tempted to make claims for tests that are well in excess of those claimed by the test designers. Speaking at a conference of British occupational psychologists in 2003, an American test salesman justified testing on the grounds that 'You do not want losers contaminating your organisations.' In the USA there is no Data Protection Act, and it is said that companies seldom offer feedback to candidates for fear of litigation. Although we understand that American psychologists offer feedback to those that they assess as a matter of routine, we also understand that American companies tend not to offer feedback to candidates for fear of litigation.

Test quality

Some tests have appeared that are either designed or endorsed by well-known psychologists or by business or other personalities. However, such associations are not always a sign of quality, and some have lacked the full range of evidence of worth that we would consider appropriate before tests are released for general use.

Graphology and other selection methods

Graphologists and others continue to claim to have selection methods at least as good as those offered by psychologists. Indeed, in 2003 one national daily newspaper in the UK appointed a resident graphologist to make regular contributions about the personality of business leaders in its business section. Elsewhere in the newspaper readers were told that graphologists had expertise to offer in bringing up children and in career choice. However, any information offered in support of these claims is usually anecdotal and falls far short of the independent predictive validation studies that can be offered as evidence of the best psychological tests.

Statistical inaccuracy

Our fifth area of concern continues to be the incorrect use of statistics to try to convince people of the worth of tests. Perhaps the most common of these is the use of the correlation matrix, in which the relationship between scores on a number of tests, and performance on a number of indicators, is summarised by a series of numbers. For example, if there are scores on nine tests, and assessments on nine performance criteria such as quality and quantity of work, a total of 81 correlations could be calculated. Once the correlations have been calculated, a high correlation between a test and a performance criterion may be offered as 'proof' of the worth of the test. However, two essential points must be taken into account when evaluating this 'proof'. The first is that when a large number of correlations are calculated, some relatively large correlations will occur by chance and the same effect may not be found if a second, independent study is carried out. This point and related issues are discussed in Appendix II. The second point to consider is that tests are normally being used long before such independent studies can be carried out. Attention must be given to how a test has been used to make selection and other decisions pending the results of the studies and then whether use will change in line with any new information.

All in all, testing is now big business, and many organisations and individuals now depend on income from test sales. One indication of this is that we were threatened with legal action in connection with a survey carried out for the Second Edition of this book. The threat was made as soon as plans for the survey were announced and before the survey methods had been decided or the results had been collected or analysed.

A related issue is that any concerns about specific tests must be expressed with extreme care because of the possibility of legal action. It is rare to have sound evidence that a test does not work – indeed, the poorer the design of the test, the less likely it is that it will have been subject to proper scientific scrutiny and review.

Against this background there must be the possibility of legislation being introduced to regulate testing. Perhaps the most likely source of this is the European Union. In general the EU has sought to harmonise policies and procedures throughout Europe, and it is clear from our survey of test publishers that there are very different views about testing in different countries in the community (see Chapter 12). It is our view that good practice in the UK should have a significant influence on any European legislation in the future.

HOW THIS BOOK IS STRUCTURED

Chapter 1 gives an overview of how tests are used in today's environment. The aim is to give busy executives and others an appreciation of both the potential benefits and the 'downsides' of testing.

Chapters 2 and 3 describe what constitutes a test and give examples of the main types of test available.

Chapter 4 discusses ethical, legal and social issues.

Chapters 5, 6, 7 and 8 deal with the related issues of obtaining tests, strategies for using tests in selection, choosing tests and introducing testing, and of making and communicating decisions.

Chapter 9 is about testing top managers.

Chapter 10 covers the evaluation of tests in times of change.

Chapter 11 looks at testing and measurement in a wider context, including other assessment tools (such as 360-degree feedback and competencies).

Chapter 12 concerns testing on the Internet and other developments. It includes the views of representatives of leading UK test publishers.

There are four Appendixes:

Appendix I gives details of leading test publishers.

Appendix II gives guidance on assessing the worth of large correlations.

Appendix III gives guidance to those taking tests and receiving feedback.

Appendix IV gives an example of an assessment report based on tests and question-naires.

We hope that this new edition will be of interest both to new and old readers. We would welcome feedback and any ideas for future editions.

John Toplis, Vic Dulewicz, Clive Fletcher
July 2004

Acknowledgements

We thank Dr Jeannette James for her contribution to earlier editions of this book, some parts of which appear again in this edition, and Helena Rozga for her comments about our final draft.

Representatives of seven leading UK test publishers were interviewed as part of our preparation of this edition (see Chapter 12) and we wish to acknowledge the willing help given by:

Professor Dave Bartram, SHL Group
Anne Biggs, ASE Solutions Limited
Wendy Lord, the Test Agency
Mac Morrisby, the Morrisby Organisation
Dr Robert McHenry, Oxford Psychologists Press Limited
Paul McKeon, the Psychological Corporation Limited
Laurence Paltiel, Psytech International Limited.

Contact details appear in Appendix I.

Throughout this book there are frequent references to the British Psychological Society, and in particular to the Psychological Testing Centre. We are grateful to the Centre for making information available to us about the numbers of people with Level A and Level B certificates of competence in occupational testing. The Society and the Testing Centre are at:

St Andrews House
48 Princess Road East
Leicester
LE17DR

Tel.: 01162 549568
www.bps.org
www.psychtesting.org.uk

1

Introduction: testing in today's environment

This book is about the kinds of tests that are widely used in the world of work. The tests are often used as part of a selection procedure, but they may also be used for other purposes, such as career counselling, staff development and team-building. The tests may be administered and interpreted by an organisation's own staff, but may be used by consultants and other advisers.

This chapter aims to give busy executives and others an appreciation of the potential benefits and 'downsides' of testing.

DIFFERENT KINDS OF TESTS

The tests described in this book are of two types.

Psychometric tests aim to measure different kinds of mental abilities. This group of tests includes reasoning and problem-solving tests. They are characterised by having answers that can be scored as 'correct' or as 'incorrect'. The scoring process often involves totalling the number of correct answers and comparing the total with those of a relevant group of people – eg graduate applicants.

By contrast, *psychometric questionnaires* aim to measure the attitudes and preferences of an individual. This group of 'tests' includes personality questionnaires. Answers are often made by agreeing or disagreeing with a statement such as 'I feel nervous before making a presentation to top managers'. Answers can thus reflect preferences or behaviour. The scoring process often involves combining the replies from similar questions into scales reflecting an individual's confidence, nervousness, etc. A profile of scores – often referred to as a 'personality profile' – may be produced.

THE BENEFITS OF TESTING

Over the years it has been shown that, at their best, psychometric tests and questionnaires can identify sales staff with the highest sales figures, production staff with the highest output figures, supervisors with the highest staff morale, etc. This makes the idea of testing attractive to employers and employees alike. For employers it is an important way of competing effectively – if they can attract the high-performing employees while leaving the others for their competitors, this may give them an important competitive edge. For employees, there can be real benefits in having strengths identified and developed; if individuals are placed in work which makes best use of their skills and abilities, and which matches their personality, interests and values, this can dramatically affect their output, their satisfaction, their earnings and their quality of life.

HOW TESTS ARE USED

Tests normally form just part of a selection procedure. However, because they are often designed so that large numbers of people can take them at relatively low cost, they often feature in one of the early stages in a selection procedure.

For example, one or more tests may be used as part of a large-scale recruitment campaign. After an initial sift of applications to make sure that applicants meet other requirements such as educational or vocational qualifications, large numbers of applicants might be tested as part of the process of deciding who should be among the relatively small numbers called to interview. Increasingly, such testing is carried out over the Internet.

In contrast, tests are sometimes used towards the end of a selection procedure as part of an in-depth assessment of the most promising candidates. In these circumstances a combination of tests and questionnaires might be used so as to give a comprehensive picture of cognitive ability, cognitive style, personality and motivation.

As well as being used as part of selection or assessment procedures, tests and questionnaires can also be used to counsel and advise people regarding their career choice and career development. And they can also be used as part of team-building exercises, from which results can shed light on preferences and styles of the team members and how they can work better together. They can be used too as a source of information about the state of an organisation's human resources and inform decisions about capability to retrain or change in other ways.

CASE STUDY 1

Taking stock of an organisation's human resources

Shortly after his appointment as personnel director of a financial services organisation, an experienced HR professional introduced short training courses for branch managers. As part of the training he asked managers to complete a short reasoning test.

Analysing the results by the years that people were promoted to branch manager, he found that the average scores had been falling in each of the ten years prior to his appointment, although the demands made on the branch managers were increasing. As a result, the procedure for identifying which staff should be promoted to management was strengthened by the introduction of tests and in other ways.

The following case studies illustrate other successful uses of tests.

CASE STUDY 2

Devising a new selection procedure

Some years ago one of the authors was asked to advise a company on how to improve its selection of supervisors. After he had collected background information, it became clear that the problem was a very real one.

Over the years the company's manufacturing process had become more complicated, demanding higher levels of diagnostic skill, staff management, recordkeeping and reporting. By contrast, selection procedures for supervisors had deteriorated. No longer were they carefully selected, trained and monitored when they supervised for the first time. Instead, those willing to help the existing supervisors had then themselves been put in charge. Several of these supervisors volunteered the information that they could not cope.

A new selection system involving a combination of psychological tests, group discussions and individual interviews brought dramatic results. Existing employees working elsewhere in the organisation were identified as having the potential to develop. As a group they excelled during training, impressing both the company training staff and external examiners. As individuals they were pleased to show what they could do, while the company was pleased to have these key vacancies filled by people of suitable calibre.

CASE STUDY 3

Assessing senior managers as part of a reorganisation

In 1991, the main part of a major UK organisation decided to reorganise, moving from one form of hierarchical structure to another. Psychometric tests and other assessment methods were commissioned from and run by external consultants to help decide which of the top managers in the old structure were best suited to the top posts in the new structure. Although the organisation already had information about its top managers from appraisal schemes and in other ways, it was felt that the additional information from the assessments made a worthwhile contribution to the placement process.

The success of the process meant that similar assessment procedures were commissioned and run when other parts of the organisation reorganised in subsequent years.

CASE STUDY 4

Assessing an individual

An applicant for the post of management consultant was asked to complete a personality questionnaire as part of the selection procedure. At interview he was well dressed and appeared extremely confident and self-assured. He talked about his business success, his family and his wide circle of friends. He was the leading figure in a local charitable organisation.

From the point of view of the interviewer, however, the impression that he was making was difficult to reconcile with the picture given by the personality questionnaire that he had completed. This suggested an individual of extreme sensitivity.

Towards the end of the interview, the personality profile was discussed with the applicant who readily agreed with the picture given by the questionnaire. He explained that on a number of occasions top managers had tried to persuade him to move into general management posts, but that he had not wished to be exposed to situations that would require such a robust personality. The applicant's self-awareness and insight was seen as a particular strength.

CASE STUDY 5

Advice on career choice

A business school graduate was involved in the strategic planning work for a major charity. Test results showed that she had good reasoning skills and that she had a thorough approach to her work. During a career review meeting she expressed her deep frustration at some of the members of the senior management team. She felt that they read her reports superficially and then quoted selectively and out of context. She decided to seek work with a charity where her work would be appreciated.

SOME DISADVANTAGES AND DANGERS

Following these examples of the successful use of tests, it is important to add that there are a large number of reasons why testing may be ineffective, unfair or both. Reasons include the following – and often there are combinations of reasons:

- The test does not meet recognised design standards.
- The test is not appropriate – for example, the content might be inappropriate, or the test might be too difficult.
- The test may be unfair to some applicants because of their sex, race or disability, or because test security has been breached
- The test may be administered incorrectly (for example, allowing too much or too little time).
- The test may be scored incorrectly; examples would be to use the wrong scoring keys,

to add scores incorrectly, or to compare an individual applicant's scores with the wrong norm group (eg comparing a graduate applicant with a group of top managers rather than other graduate entrants). The test result may be interpreted incorrectly – for example, it is sometimes assumed (incorrectly) that a person who likes working with numbers will be quick and accurate at figure-work, and that a person who does not like working with numbers will be slow or inaccurate.

To be successful, all the above stages in a selection process have to be satisfactory. The following case studies illustrate problems with particular stages.

CASE STUDY 6

Test not meeting recognised design standards

A major computer company felt that it should be able to supply customers with an aptitude test so that the customers could recruit good-quality programmers and other staff. A test was purchased from consultants by one of its overseas subsidiaries and circulated to Head Office staff in London.

At this stage one of us saw the test and recognised the test items – they had been copied from different pages of a well-known textbook on psychological testing, where they had been used to illustrate the different kinds of psychological tests that are available. It is important to note that there is a chance that a test like this might work and that we did not have any evidence that it did not. Yet its origins did not give confidence that it would be effective and that it would not discriminate unfairly.

CASE STUDY 7

Inappropriate use of a test

In order to attract trainees, a private computer programming school offered potential students the opportunity to take an aptitude test to check whether they had the ability to succeed in a course. A large number passed, enrolled and paid their fees, but many found it difficult to find employment at the end of the course.

It emerged that the test was originally designed for data-preparation staff and that the standards required to pass the test were less demanding than those required for programming work.

CASE STUDY 8

Breach of test security

Some years ago, one of the authors was asked to review the effectiveness of a test of dexterity that was being used to select operatives on an assembly line. The test involved screw threads, washers and nuts, and the task appeared similar to the work being done on the line itself. Those who completed the selection task in the fastest times were selected.

However, analysis of the test scores showed that the job performance of those with the highest test scores was actually poorer than the job performance of those with lower test scores. We then heard a rumour that some of the more enterprising employees had copied the test, and that relatives and friends were practising the test at a nearby house before presenting themselves for selection.

Incorrect interpretation

As part of a major reorganisation, tests were used within an assessment procedure for over 300 existing managers to help decide on their allocation to positions in the new organisation. It was widely known that some staff would be surplus and that voluntary redundancy was a possibility. The size of the assessment programme and the speed with which the exercise had to be carried out meant that a number of independent consultants were recruited on a contract basis to give feedback about performance on the psychological tests that had been used, and to write a report on each manager based on discussion of the manager's performance during the assessment procedure as a whole. These reports were to be fed back to the managers, both to explain the reasons for the decisions made and to help them to plan their future.

Although all the consultants had attended the short training courses run by the suppliers of the psychological tests, major problems were found in their written reports dealing with the tests as well as the parts dealing with the rest of the procedure.

A special team of chartered psychologists had to be recruited to rewrite the reports before they could be circulated.

By this stage we hope that readers will realise that although the concept of testing is relatively easy to grasp, the subject is potentially complex. For example, a choice of several thousand tests is now available, although in practice a few tests are widely used and others remain merely catalogue items. If you are a manager, you have only a few choices.

- Ignore the subject: you may take the view that selecting the best staff does not matter – but there are clear differences in the performance of employees, and if you employ the poor performers you will be at a significant disadvantage against your competitors (Schmidt and Hunter, 1998). Alternatively, you may take the view that you will simply dismiss those recruits who do not meet your standards – however, Schmidt and Hunter say that in their experience supervisors are reluctant to terminate the employment of marginal performers because doing so is an unpleasant experience for them.

- Leave the matter to someone else in your organisation. For example, testing and other forms of assessment now form part of the studies of members of the Chartered Institute of Personnel and Development (CIPD), and some CIPD-qualified staff go on to be trained in the use of one or more tests. Training in testing can be expensive, and it does not make sense for every manager in an organisation to be trained.

- Get trained in testing. If you decide on this option, we would strongly recommend that you attend training that qualifies you for the certificates of competence in psychological testing issued by the British Psychological Society. Training of this kind will help you to evaluate the many possible tests available, to decide which may be of value in your organisation, to ensure that they are used and interpreted correctly, and to show you how to check on the value and fairness of the tests.

- Seek advice from consultants. We would strongly advise you to seek advice from chartered occupational psychologists with certificates of competence in psychological testing. In contrast we are concerned about the availability and use of some tests administered on the Internet from overseas locations.

To complete this overview, questions that are frequently asked about tests (and some answers) include:

Q *Are psychological tests available for every job?*
A No. There are too many different jobs for that to be possible. However, some tests cover groups of related jobs, such as those involving different types of sales work. Others cover skills that occur in many jobs, such as clerical checking or interpreting graphs and tables correctly. If no 'off-the-shelf' tests are available, remember when hiring applicants without experience for a wide range of jobs, a test of 'general mental ability' (a test of reasoning or general cognitive ability) is likely to be the most valid single predictor (Schmidt and Hunter, 1998). However, for specialist jobs it may be appropriate to design and use tailor-made tests if the numbers of applicants and vacancies warrant the costs that will be incurred.

Q *So why not use tests in every selection procedure?*
A For a number of reasons, several of which may be relevant in a particular situation. Some of the more common objections to testing are:

- the cost (not just the cost of the test materials, but of attending training courses in testing and the absence from other work) – However, the benefits of testing can be considerably greater than the costs – an unsatisfactory chief executive can ruin an organisation!

- the effect on candidates – It is sometimes said (i) that candidates will object to being tested, particularly if they have professional or other qualifications, or (ii) that candidates will object to taking part in a procedure that becomes long and demanding because of the inclusion of tests. However, in our experience such objections are seldom raised by people who see themselves as good candidates and who are normally keen to show what they can do

- resistance from existing employees – Some existing employees may take the view that selection from existing staff should be based on seniority alone. There can also be pressures to recruit relations and friends of existing managers and employees without other criteria being taken into account. However, it is our view that both kinds of pressure must be resisted if organisations are to be competitive and efficient

- because tests may discriminate unfairly – But any part of a selection procedure may discriminate unfairly, and it cannot be assumed either that tests will discriminate unfairly or that they will be the part of the selection process most likely to discriminate. Further, because test administration and scoring are standardised and objective (see Chapter 2), tests may be more consistent in their fairness than are relatively subjective methods, such as the interview.

Q *How can tests predict performance?*
A Different kinds of tests predict different aspects of future performance. For example:

- Aptitude tests involve a series of similar items, such as checking figures or understanding paragraphs of information. Such tests can be a useful guide to what people are able to do and what skills they might develop.

- Trainability tests involve giving candidates a short period of intensive training after which their performance is assessed and any errors of technique noted. As the name implies, the tests can be a useful guide to training-course performance in particular.

- Personality questionnaires focus on aspects of the personality of candidates – for example, the way they tend to relate to other people and how they feel about themselves.

- Questionnaires about attitudes and values explore yet other aspects of candidates.

Q *What kind of pay-off can I expect from tests?*
A Pay-off must take account of both benefits (eg reducing the turnover of staff and/or recruiting new staff whose productivity is higher) and costs. It depends not only on the extent of the improvement in the selection method but also on the numbers of people involved. Follow-up studies can be difficult and time-consuming, and in our experience are relatively rare – however, one study in 1986 estimated annual net savings of over £1.3 million (see Chapter 10).

Q *Is one kind of test likely to be better than another?*
A Although a major review by Schmidt and Hunter (1998) suggested a test of 'general mental ability' might be the best single predictor of subsequent performance (see Chapter 3), it is clear that no single test (or other selection method) will provide perfect predictions of job perform-ance. For example, one individual may be motivated to make full use of his or her intelligence or general cognitive ability, while another with an identical test score may not be motivated or may be distracted by other things. The same authors also found that a work sample test could be the best single predictor of performance for those applicants with previous experience. So there is no simple rule of thumb, and attention has now turned to finding the best combination of selection methods for each particular situation.

Q *Once testing is started in an organisation, how do you know when to stop?*
A In general, testing will contribute most when recruiting new people or when filling new kinds of vacancies for which existing staff have little or no experience. Whatever the reason for test-ing, test results must be integrated with other human resource systems and processes, such as information from performance appraisals and development reviews. In some organisations, competencies are used to describe job requirements and tests are used as a source of infor-mation about some or all of the competencies (see Chapter 11). In this way, relatively objective information can be built up about an organisation's human resources and its potential for development and change. However, tests are not the only method of assessment, and they should not be used unless the results 'add value' to the information that already exists. Further, feedback should be available to those who have been tested, just as they should be able to dis-cuss the results of their annual appraisal.

Q *I am interested in better selection but it all sounds rather complicated. What is the best way forward?*
A Read this book to get some background information. Then reflect on any current problems that you may have in recruiting and selecting staff. For example, do you have a group of staff whose performance has been poor and/or whose turnover is high, and could better selection help to remedy this? If you think it might, why not contact an occupational psychologist for a professional opinion? The British Psychological Society produces a *Directory of Chartered Psychologists* which details the services that they offer. This information can also be accessed online at the British Psychological Society's website (www.bps.org.uk).

Q *I am suspicious of experts – particularly psychologists! Can't we just buy some tests and get on with it?*
A If you ask around or search the Internet you will be able to get hold of what appear to be tests and 'get on with it'. But bear in mind that tests cannot be judged by appearance alone. For example, a questionnaire recently sold to managers to help them assess personality was put to scientific investigation and found to be of no value. Indeed, it is not unknown for unsuitable tests to select the people who will do least well. Rather than run the risk of adding to your costs without getting any benefits, why not do the job properly and seek appropriate information from the British Psychological Society and the Chartered Institute of Personnel and Development?

Q *But surely the chances of being misled are small?*
A There is a great deal of money to be made from selection methods, and none of the consultants or others selling techniques for assessing staff lack confidence in their products. Among the methods used to impress potential clients are:

- charging very large fees (anything costing that much must be the ultimate selection method!)

- charging low fees and relying on a high volume of sales ('You don't need psychologists and expensive training courses – here is something that is practical and self-explanatory!')

- the production of testimonials from well-known personalities (any selection method will get it right sometimes, just as a clock that is not working will be correct once in every 12 hours – so do the testimonials come from people who are expert in the evaluation of selection methods?)

- the inclusion of guidelines and other information from professional societies (the quotations may be selective and the full guidelines may not be followed by those selling the tests)

- the production of lists of references to publications and articles (remember that the best scientific and professional journals have an editorial advisory panel of experts to help to check the worth of claims made; in contrast, other journals and magazines may not seek such technical advice and may be interested only in articles likely to increase their circulation)

- the production of books that endorse the technique or approach (again, sales may have been the main editorial consideration)

- the idea that the technique can reveal 'the truth' about the candidate, getting behind what the candidate would wish to be known and perhaps revealing information unknown even to the candidate (the origins of 'the truth' may be the time and date of birth of the candidate, appearance, body movements and gestures, handwriting, and so on); often the need for training in the techniques is emphasised

- an emphasis on the need for training in relation to other techniques, including those that may originate from, or be associated with, clinical psychology (again, the appeal of such techniques is the belief that they will help to reveal 'the truth')

- the offer of a free trial of the methods, usually involving the person who will decide whether or not the technique will be used (the consultants are obtaining a degree of commitment by the trial itself: whatever the picture given, few are likely to argue with it – see Chapter 5)

- the production of spurious scientific evidence – many managers do not understand the key terms 'reliability' and 'validity' which are used in the assessment of selection procedures, and this lack of knowledge can be exploited. For example, managers may relax simply because these key words have been used, and not check that they have been used properly. The effect may be compounded if statistics are added – fewer still can judge whether the statistics are appropriate. Remember that it is always possible to make calculations of the key figures of reliability and validity – what matters is the source of the data, the results obtained and their statistical significance, which in turn reflects the sample sizes involved (see Chapters 2 and 10)

- presenting the methods well (it seems to add to the credibility of the procedure if, for example, the assessment involves the use of a computer connected to the Internet, and the results can be presented on a computer printout and/or in the form of a profile).

The 'sales' methods described above are often used in combination, so the offer of a test or tests might be backed by the claim that they are supported by psychologists, references to research, links to the British Psychological Society, etc. But remember that if a chartered psychologist were to be associated with an organisation supplying tests to those without Level A or B certificates of competence, he or she would be liable to disciplinary action by the British Psychological Society – which could result in the loss of chartered status.

Because many reputable psychological tests also have at least some of the above characteristics, it is virtually impossible for the untrained manager to distinguish between selection methods that are valid and those that are not. For this reason, many well-known industrial and other organisations are currently using unproven methods.

2

Characteristics of tests

Independent evaluation has shown that well-designed psychological tests can make an important contribution to selection procedures. However, there are many 'tests' around which are not well designed but for which the same benefits are claimed.

To help readers to discriminate between the genuine articles and the pseudo-tests, this chapter begins with a brief history of psychological tests and goes on to introduce the characteristics and technical features of tests and questionnaires that meet accepted professional standards. These standards are maintained by the British Psychological Society through its guidelines for training courses in the use of tests and its evaluation processes.

A BRIEF HISTORY OF PSYCHOLOGICAL TESTING

Psychological tests are not, as some people believe, a new and questionable device imported from the USA. It is well over 100 years since Sir Francis Galton, a cousin of Charles Darwin, published *Inquiries into Human Faculty and its Development*, and over 100 years since Munsterberg used tests to select tram drivers in Austria. At the beginning of the twentieth century, Binet, a Frenchman, constructed the first intelligence test, a forerunner of today's ability tests.

Personality questionnaires have been around almost as long. The first such instrument used as a selection tool was Woodworth's Personal Data Sheet, a rough screening device for identifying seriously neurotic men who would be unfit for the American Army during World War I. Indeed, the two world wars provided a major impetus in testing, recruiters on both sides of the Atlantic being faced with a massive need for assessments, and very little time. Tests and questionnaires were used to allocate men to posts most appropriate to their abilities, and as part of the procedure to select officers.

Following World War II there was steady growth in the use of tests in the USA in both the public sector and by private organisations. However, in the early 1960s the growth was checked because of stringent equal opportunities legislation, and fear of court action while the legal situation was clarified. Subsequently, there appears to have been a resurgence of interest and application. At the last count there were more than 5,000 psychological instruments produced in the English language alone, but the vast majority of these are available for use by qualified psychologists only, and in other settings such as educational and clinical psychology.

Past research into the costs and benefits of selection has shown that major benefits can result from testing. After World War II the main test users in the United Kingdom were the Forces, the Civil Service and some large public corporations, although more recently significant numbers of private organisations have also used tests quite extensively. In both the UK and the USA a considerable increase in test usage by the private sector has been apparent over the last 20 years, particularly with the advent of testing over the Internet during the last five years. In a survey of methods used for managerial, professional and skilled manual selection conducted by the CIPD (*Recruitment Survey Report*, May 2001), 60 per cent of respondents used tests of specific skills, 55 per cent used general ability tests, 45 per cent used literacy and numeracy tests, and 41 per cent used personality questionnaires.

WHAT IS A PSYCHOLOGICAL TEST?

The British Psychological Society (BPS) has a key role in controlling the publication of professionally produced test materials. The BPS has provided the following useful definition of a test:

> *The term 'psychological test' refers to a procedure for the evaluation of psychological functions. Psychological tests involve those being tested in solving problems, performing skilled tasks or making judgements. Psychological test procedures are characterised by standard methods of administration and scoring. Results are usually quantified by means of normative or other scaling procedures [these terms are explained later in this chapter] but they may also be interpreted qualitatively by reference to psychological theory. Included in the term 'psychological test' are tests of varieties of: intelligence; ability; aptitude; language development and function; perception; personality; temperament and disposition; and interests, habits, values and preferences.*

The BPS definition thus embraces a wide range of tests and questionnaires under the overall heading of 'psychological tests'. This book concentrates on those instruments that are available to non-psychologists and for which training is available – however, other instruments that are of value in occupational assessment but that can be used only by accredited psychologists are mentioned from time to time.

PROPERTIES OF PSYCHOLOGICAL TESTS WHICH MEET ACCEPTED PROFESSIONAL STANDARDS

This section deals with the fundamentals of psychological tests that distinguish them from the plethora of other paper-and-pencil instruments used in personnel and training departments. It is important to draw attention to these distinctions: tests and questionnaires that are not professionally designed can be similar in appearance and design – indeed, they are sometimes called 'psychological' or said to be based on psychological theory, perhaps in the hope of increasing sales.

In this book we propose to break down the term 'psychological tests' and to distinguish between psychometric tests and psychometric questionnaires. Cronbach (1984) has proposed a useful distinction between tests of *maximum performance* – eg mental ability tests – and tests of habitual or *typical performance* – eg personality questionnaires.

Tests of *maximum performance* usually measure intelligence or special abilities, and have correct answers so that, broadly speaking, the higher the score, the better the performance. As a group, such tests are described as 'psychometric tests' during the remainder of this book when specific reference is necessary.

In contrast, tests of *typical performance* (questionnaires) tend to be designed to measure personality characteristics, interests, values or behaviour, and therefore an ability is not being stretched to get a high score. With questionnaires, a high or a low 'score' signifies the extent to which a person possesses qualities such as co-operation or determination, and the appropriateness of the replies will depend on the vacancy to be filled. Some questionnaires measure bi-polar scales, such as introversion-extraversion; replies indicate an individual's position on the scale. As a group, such tests are described as 'psychometric questionnaires' during the remainder of this book whenever necessary.

Well-designed psychometric tests often share six properties:

- objective, standardised measurement
- the test items are ordered by level of ability
- objective scoring
- interpretation using 'norms'
- technical manuals
- objective evidence of validity.

Objective, standardised measurement

With a few exceptions that are beyond the scope of this book, tests are objective, standardised measures – they require a highly controlled, uniform procedure for administration and scoring. For every candidate the test items and instructions should be the same; the time allowed should be the same if it is a timed test; the physical test conditions should be the same – ie adequate lighting, a comfortable temperature, no distractions whatsoever, plenty of work space; and so on.

Test items ordered by level of ability

In their pencil-and-paper form, a second feature of proper ability and other psychometric tests is that the test items will be ordered in level of difficulty so that candidates can get settled into the test more easily, and weaker candidates are not faced with overly complex items early on – they have an opportunity to demonstrate what they are able to do. The difficulty level is determined objectively during the pilot (design) stage of construction by calculating the percentage of those taking the test who got an item correct. In the final versions of the tests, items are re-ordered according to these percentages so that, for example, an item that 95 per cent of the pilot sample got correct would be placed very early on, whereas an item which was answered correctly by only 5 per cent of the sample would come very close to the end. In this way, when there are time limits, only people with a very high ability at this type of problem-solving are faced with such a difficult item.

With the advent of testing on computers (whether involving a standalone PC or testing over the Internet) the underlying models of testing have changed. By making continual assessments of accuracy and of the time taken to complete items, candidates are offered a series of questions tailored to their level of ability. In this so-called 'adaptive' testing each person being tested is presented with a unique combination of questions so that his or her chances of success for each item are around 50 per cent (see Chapter 12).

Objective scoring

Third, psychometric tests and questionnaires are usually scored objectively. The administrator (or the computer program) has a key which contains the right answers for the test, or the value to be given to a specific answer on a multiple-choice questionnaire. Thus, with objectively scored instruments, the scorer's judgement does not lead to variations in score (see Chapter 12).

Interpretation using 'norms'

A fourth major determinant of objectivity and standardisation is the way in which a score is interpreted. The number of correct items on an ability test, or the sum of values for responses on a questionnaire scale, constitutes a raw score which has significance only when it is compared to the range of scores obtained from a large representative sample of people for whom the test was designed. The sample might be drawn from the general population or from more specific groups – such as UK graduates or craft apprentices – and is known as the standardisation sample. The results constitute norms which, as the name implies, relate all scores to the normal or average performance of the group, and the degrees of deviation above and below the average. It is important that precise information is given about the way that the norms were drawn up – for example, norms for 'supervisors' could be based on those working as supervisors, those appointed as supervisors, those called to a selection procedure for supervisors, or all applicants for supervisory work.

A normative score is obtained by comparison with a norms table and is not open to subjective interpretation. The most widely used normative scale is the percentile score, which is a rank order scale reflecting the proportion of the reference group who obtained a lower score than the individual being tested. So if a graduate applicant scored at the 65th percentile on a particular test, using UK graduate norms, his score would be better than 65 per cent of UK graduates (see Chapter 7).

Technical manuals

Psychometric instruments should have manuals or other reference materials that contain scientific, objective data to demonstrate how good the test is, and to what extent it does what it is supposed to do. Two critical concepts are the test's *reliability* and *validity*. *Reliability* refers to the stability and consistency of results obtained, and it can be assessed in several different ways. In the 'test-retest' method of assessing reliability a large group of people is tested and then retested, using the same test, several weeks later. The initial experience of doing the test is likely to improve the group performance on the second occasion. However, if the relative positions of individual scores are found to be very different on the two occasions, the reliability of the test would be suspect.

A good test manual contains empirical evidence of the test-retest reliability, showing the degree of similarity between the results obtained from the first and second administration of the tests to the same sample, and also the degree of internal consistency, using the split half method. This involves comparing the scores obtained on one half of the items (normally the odd-numbered items) to the scores obtained on the other half (the even-numbered items). This figure will reflect the internal consistency of the test – ie whether or not its items all measure the same broad characteristic.

During the design stage of a reputable psychometric instrument, great care is taken to ensure that only the items that are measuring the same broad ability are retained for a specific scale. As part of this process, attention must be paid to the way in which the questions are presented. For example, if some of a trial group were to get all the items of a similar format wrong, it would be a sign that these items might be measuring a separate ability, and this possibility would have to be checked (see Chapter 7).

Objective evidence of validity

Validity is undoubtedly the most important single issue when choosing a test for occupational assessment, and it is a measure of how far the test measures what it was designed to measure. In the occupational context, validity is usually demonstrated by relating the score on a test given prior to employment to some sort of external measure of work performance – eg appraisal ratings of job performance, quasi-objective measures such as sales figures or ratings of performance on a training course, where successful completion of the course is a prerequisite for job success. If the performance measure is obtained some time after the test has been taken, the validity measure that can be calculated is the *predictive validity*. This is the extent to which a test can predict future behaviour because it takes account of the wide range of factors that a job incumbent is exposed to, and is influenced by. Predictive validity is regarded as the best single measure of the worth of a test.

There are often a number of practical reasons – especially time pressure – why it is not possible to do a predictive validation study, and so a concurrent study (in which the test and performance measures are taken at the same time by existing staff) has to suffice. Although *concurrent validity* gives a fairly good indication of the relevance of a test to work performance, it is not as good a measure as predictive validity because the test performance of existing staff may be affected by skills and other behaviours acquired during the current employment rather than aptitude or trainability.

Two other types of validity are sometimes referred to, especially if concurrent or predictive evidence is not available. *Content validity* relates to how comprehensively the total field or domain of the target trait or construct has been covered by the items. For example, a test of extraversion should cover items related to outgoingness, assertiveness, social-boldness, social enthusiasm, and group-orientation. If items do not cover all domains, the test is not comprehensive and therefore does not have content validity. *Construct validity* deals with how well, or to what degree, the test measures the target trait or construct. This is usually evaluated by correlating scores on the new test with scores on other, well-validated tests, which measure the same, or part of, the construct or trait.

When selecting a psychometric test or questionnaire for a specific purpose, the most important data in the manual are those relating to validity. People involved in test selection should look to see if the instrument shows good validity data on a group of employees similar to the one that is to be assessed. Avoid reliance on job titles alone because they can be misleading – for example, in organisations like the Civil Service and Post Office, 'executive-grade staff' are middle managers rather than top managers. Ideally, the number involved in the validation study should be at least 100 and the correlation between test scores and the criteria of performance should be at least 0.2 (see Chapter 7). If the correlation is lower, it is unlikely that the use of the test will be financially worthwhile (see Chapters 7 and 10).

One final issue on validity is that of *face validity*, which refers to the extent to which the instrument looks as if it is measuring something relevant to the job. Unfortunately, psychometric tests and questionnaires are sometimes judged only on their appearances, and because the computer graphics and graphic design of some unproven 'tests' can be at least as good as the best of the proven tests, errors of judgement can be made. Face validity is nevertheless of some importance – if an instrument has a low face validity or contains items which might, for example, appear bizarre or intrusive to respondents, then its acceptability to candidates will be questionable, and this might well affect their motivation and hence undermine the validity of the results. For example, the use of an 'inkblots' test on graduates or managers often arouses reactions of mirth, irritation or even hostility, and can affect their attitude not only to the specific test but to the entire test procedure. Moreover, lack of face validity can also be a disadvantage in the context of legal challenges to test use (see Chapter 7).

Information on face validity does not usually appear in psychometric test and questionnaire manuals. In this matter, users have to exercise their own judgement about the potential suitability of an instrument to a particular group of employees. One way around this problem (and another problem when it is not possible to validate an instrument) is to look for an instrument that measures the same characteristic (as denoted by a statistically significant correlation) as another that has already been shown to be valid on a similar group. Most manuals contain the correlations between the test or questionnaire and other similar instruments. If the new instrument is more acceptable, and correlates highly with the unacceptable one, this can be used in its place with some confidence. Nevertheless, a specific validation study should still be set up wherever possible (see Chapter 10).

For a more detailed treatment of the nature and construction of psychological tests, see Anastasi (1998, 6th edition) or Kline (1998).

In summary, a 'true' psychometric test or questionnaire can be distinguished in the following ways:

- It is supplied by a reputable publisher of test materials only to those who have received training in its use.
- It is supplied with instructions for administration, scoring and interpretation (including norms).
- It is supplied with details of its reliability and validity.

In addition, the face validity of an instrument can be important in determining its acceptability both to the candidates and to others who have to endorse the selection process and make use of information arising from it. Under normal circumstances, managers should use only 'true' tests. When this is not possible or practicable, they should retain an occupational psychologist to identify, trial and evaluate possible new tests.

THE AVAILABILITY OF PSYCHOLOGICAL TESTS

'True' tests are carefully designed and developed, and unless they are used by people who are fully qualified or at least adequately trained, their value is strictly limited and their security jeopardised. The British Psychological Society, with the assistance and full support of the reputable test suppliers, has sought to maintain standards.

People who want to use reputable test materials must complete special courses. Training in the use of tests of *maximum performance* (Level A tests of ability or aptitude) normally takes about a week, and constitutes an entry requirement for further courses in the use of tests of *typical performance* (Level B personality and interest questionnaires). A generic course in the latter also lasts about one week, although some providers offer courses in a modular format. Courses are designed and run by chartered occupational psychologists, who are individually responsible to the BPS for their technical standards and scope of the course. Attendance on these courses is a major stepping-stone towards the attainment of a certificate of competence for Level A and Level B tests, awarded by the BPS. Further details of courses and BPS certificates appear in Chapter 4.

Finally, a cautionary point should be made. Attendance at any Level A or Level B course is a necessary, but not sufficient, condition for ordering and using any test at a given level. Test publishers usually require some additional training for their tests if the tester has not attended one of their training courses. Further details on how to obtain tests and to become trained and accredited to use them are provided in Chapter 5.

Tests and questionnaires that are available over the Internet without these training requirements do not conform to accepted professional guidelines and should be avoided (see Chapter 12).

3

Types of tests and outline descriptions

The aim of this chapter is to outline the kinds of tests that are most commonly used in selection and, where appropriate, their origins in psychology. Detailed reviews of leading tests can be obtained from the British Psychological Society's Psychological Testing Centre. Details of some of the reputable publishers who specialise in psychological test materials are given in Appendix I.

At this stage we do not discuss the testing medium – most tests started life in pencil-and-paper format, but now many can be administered on personal computers or even over the Internet (see Chapter 12).

Psychometric tests of *maximum performance* are divided into:

- tests of attainment
- tests of general intelligence
- tests of special ability or aptitude –
  - (i)   tests for special aptitude/ability
  - (ii) tests of aptitude for specific types of work/job
  - (iii) test batteries.

Psychometric questionnaires measuring *typical performance* can take the form of:

- self-report personality questionnaires
- emotional intelligence questionnaires
- interest questionnaires
- values questionnaires.
- work behaviour questionnaires.

In addition, five other approaches to personality assessment are described in outline, with references for further reading. These are:

- simulation/situational tests
- projective techniques
- objective tests of personality

- fringe methods of personality assessment
- integrity tests.

Finally in this chapter there is comment on using tests and questionnaires in combination.

PSYCHOMETRIC TESTS OF MAXIMUM PERFORMANCE

As just noted, there are various broad types of tests of mental ability (*maximum performance*) available: general intelligence tests, tests of special aptitude or ability, tests of aptitude for specific jobs, and tests of attainment or proficiency.

Tests of attainment

Tests of attainment – which incidentally are not included in the BPS definition of a test (above) but have similar properties and are widely used – are designed to measure the degree of knowledge and/or skill a person has acquired at a particular point in time. School examinations are one type of such a test. They are very much concerned with experience and learning, and the level of proficiency acquired at certain tasks or skills.

Tests of intelligence or aptitude, on the other hand, are designed in theory to provide a measure of an individual's capacity to learn (knowledge and skills) or to perform a skilled task in the future, irrespective of present training and experience. In practice, however, because such tests are based upon tasks incorporating verbal, numerical or symbolic information, they rarely, if ever, provide measures that are completely uninfluenced by previous experience and education. It is perhaps helpful to envisage a continuum, with pure attainment tests on one side, say on the left, and pure psychological tests of aptitude on the other, on the right. A test of mathematical attainment involving knowledge of basic mathematical principles would thus lie to the left of centre, and an A-level maths exam might lie a little further to the left, but neither would be at the end, because the person's numerical reasoning ability would also affect performance on these attainment tests. Similarly, a numerical reasoning test would lie to the right of the continuum, but not quite at the extreme because knowledge and experience of working with figures at school would probably have some effect on performance.

Psychometric tests are therefore designed to assess capacity rather than existing knowledge and skill. To give an understanding of the different types of tests of intelligence, special aptitudes or abilities and tests of aptitudes for specific jobs, examples will be described in sections below. Examples will also be given of the more widely used tests that have proved to be valuable for assessment and counselling purposes. Some tests are designed for use with the general population, to discriminate across the entire ability range, whereas others are designed to discriminate most effectively within specific sections of the range – for example, among graduate or management populations. In tests designed for the latter groups the types of mental operations called for are of a much higher order of complexity, such as reasoning and evaluation (described below). When considering tests it is important to look at the tests and the test manuals and not make decisions only on the basis of the test title. In particular, most tests have instructions that demand knowledge of language, and it is, for example, difficult to design numerical items free of verbal skills.

Tests can be used either alone or in combination with other tests according to the quality or qualities to be measured. Combinations of tests are called 'test batteries'. Some test batteries comprise tests that have been designed for use together and that may have similar instructions, ways of arriving at answers, etc. Often a single manual gives details about all the tests in the battery and features information about combinations of the tests to be used for common vacancies, such as those for apprentices or graduate entrants. Following a review of the different broad types of test, test batteries are considered further.

Tests of general intelligence

There is a multitude of different definitions of intelligence, but the simplest and most appropriate for practical purposes is 'the capacity for abstract thinking and reasoning with a range of different contents and media'. The specific scientific identification and measurement of intelligence is carried out using a statistical technique called factor analysis, to determine the general intelligence component across a number of different tests. In the 1940s, British psychologists – notably Burt and Vernon – proposed a hierarchical structure of human abilities, with the 'g', or general intelligence factor, accounting for most variation in performance across different tests. Once the effects of 'g' have been accounted for, it is possible to find two broad (major) groups of abilities:

- v:ed – standing for 'verbal and educational', and covering minor group factors such as verbal, numerical, memory and reasoning abilities
- k:m – representing spatial (after El Kousi, an Egyptian psychologist) and mechanical abilities, as well as perceptual (sensory) and motor skills relating to physical operations such as eye-hand coordination and manual dexterity.

Once the effect of these three higher-level factors have been accounted for, one is left with factors that are highly test-specific. The 'g' scores are very important for assessing someone's abilities to perform a broad range of jobs, or jobs requiring high intelligence (and also capacity to benefit from special kinds of education – eg the 11+ exam), whereas scores on minor group factors are more important for assessing people for specific jobs.

US psychologists, on the other hand, to some extent as a result of their experience of using the early intelligence tests, used different factor analytic methods in their research, which tended to emphasise differences between mental ability factors. In 1938 Thurstone identified seven ability factors that were relatively independent, although there were modest correlations between them. He named these factors 'primary mental abilities':

- spatial ability
- perceptual speed
- numerical ability
- verbal meaning
- memory
- verbal fluency
- inductive reasoning.

The model of human abilities devised by the US psychologist Guilford in the 1960s has probably had a significant influence on contemporary test constructors on both sides of the Atlantic. This model has three dimensions:

- mental operations – with five components
- products – with six components
- contents – with four components.

In the model, tests have been sought to measure each cell across the three dimensions – eg a memory test dealing with classes of objects of a semantic (ie verbal) nature, and so on. At the time of his death, Guilford had claimed to have identified 98 factors out of the total possible 120 permutations across the three dimensions. His main influence on contemporary British test constructors has been in the development of tests involving different operations, relating to various ability levels of applicants; on the important differences between convergent (problem-solving) and divergent (lateral, creative) thinking; and on the clarification of 'products' and 'contents' measured by different tests.

It usually takes between 30 and 60 minutes to obtain a reliable measure of general intelligence. Most intelligence (and aptitude) tests are administered to groups, require written responses and are timed. Items are usually presented in verbal, numerical and symbolic/diagrammatic form, thus sampling a range of different formats. The written response most commonly involves marking one of a number of possible correct answers, but a few tests require candidates to write the correct answer (these are known as open-ended). Examples of the more popular types of item format in tests of general intelligence are given below.

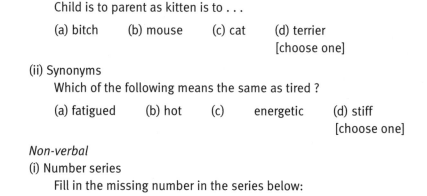

Verbal
(i) Analogies
  Child is to parent as kitten is to . . .

  (a) bitch   (b) mouse   (c) cat   (d) terrier
                                            [choose one]

(ii) Synonyms
  Which of the following means the same as tired ?

  (a) fatigued   (b) hot   (c)   energetic   (d) stiff
                                                        [choose one]

Non-verbal
(i) Number series
  Fill in the missing number in the series below:

  2   4   7   11   . . .   22

(ii) Diagrammatic/symbolic reasoning
  Which of the following should be added to complete the series of diagrams shown
  on page 22: 1, 2 or 3?

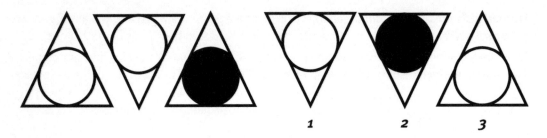

Some psychometric tests contain all these types of items, and others as well, whereas some so-called 'culture fair' tests contain only symbolic or diagrammatic items in an attempt to overcome the problems associated with candidates from different, non-Western cultures and/or those whose first language is not English. This is a major issue in testing and is examined in Chapter 4.

There are a wide variety of tests of general intelligence available, and the choice of which one to use depends largely on the educational level of applicants, their previous experience, and the jobs for which they are being considered.

Some tests are designed for individuals with average ability and are suitable for general personnel selection. However, if the need arises to assess the general intelligence of clearly above-average individuals such as graduates, managers and research staff, other tests are more suitable.

Tests of special ability or aptitude

From the early years of intelligence testing some psychologists have considered that important information about an individual's ability is obscured by concentrating on only one score – of general intelligence – and have looked at candidates' performance on specific types of items such as verbal or numerical questions (see above). This trend was accelerated by Thurstone's identification of the seven primary mental abilities. For many years, test developers have concentrated their efforts on producing tests that measure and produce a single score for a specific mental ability which is statistically reasonably independent of other special abilities. Such scores are not completely independent of each other because the influence of general intelligence also contributes to varying degrees – depending on the actual test – to a special ability score.

The terms 'special ability' and 'special aptitude' are often used imprecisely and interchangeably. A 'special aptitude' is a capacity for performing a specific group of tasks that have been shown statistically to be highly related to each other. The term 'special ability' is often used in the same sense, based upon its use in the theories of mental ability of both Thurstone and Vernon, where ability for special tasks is contrasted with general intellectual ability across all mental tasks. There are also aptitude tests for specific types of work, such as computer programming, which often combine different subtests of special abilities to provide an overall score that reflects the capacity to do a specific type of work. Examples of aptitude tests for specific types of jobs are described below and are classified both by content – ie verbal, numerical, spatial, diagrammatic/symbolic – and by level – ie for lower-level and higher-level ability.

Types of tests for special aptitude/ability
(i) Verbal ability

There are a number of tests that measure lower levels of verbal (word) meaning and comprehension, some of which also necessitate an element of reasoning with words. Verbal tests involving significantly more complex mental operations of reasoning and critical evaluation are available for assessing candidates of high ability such as graduates and managers.

(ii) Numerical ability

Lower-level numerical tests often involve an understanding of, and skill at, arithmetical calculations, and so candidates' existing attainments are being assessed as well as their aptitude. As with the verbal tests, there are also numerical tests for candidates of high ability such as graduates and potential or actual supervisors and managers. These tests assess higher-order numerical reasoning and critical evaluation of quantitative information.

(iii) Spatial ability

Candidates are required to work mentally to identify, visualise, compare and/or manipulate two- or three-dimensional shapes. Such ability has a lower general intelligence component than many of the other abilities and is therefore a more distinct, purer ability. Some tests for higher-ability candidates include three-dimensional shapes.

(iv) Diagrammatic ability

These tests do not include verbal or numerical items but include abstract symbols and diagrams, covering a range of operations from fairly superficial perceptual to complex abstract, logical processes. Some designers argue that they are not dependent on attainment and so are purer measures of reasoning, but it is debatable whether they are 'culture free' or 'culture fair'. We will return to this complex argument later.

Other tests are more appropriate for higher-ability candidates, such as technicians, scientists and software engineers:

(v) Mechanical ability

This ability incorporates an element of intelligence and reasoning and is entirely separate from manual dexterity (see below). Inevitably, there is a knowledge component (elementary physics) so the tests are not pure ability tests, but manuals do include evidence that they provide a measure of the capacity to learn and to succeed at certain jobs requiring mechanical ability and hence are tests of aptitude.

(vi) Manual dexterity

Eye-hand coordination is obviously relevant to most manual tasks, and research has shown that these abilities are not closely related to intelligence or to the abilities listed above. Indeed, there is a range of such fairly specific abilities requiring perception and manipulation involving fingers and hands. Some tasks require speed and little precision, whereas with others extreme precision is of paramount importance. Because such abilities are specific, it is necessary to carry out a careful analysis of the job before deciding which test is most appropriate. Many successful tests are actually more akin to job samples or job simulations, although a few dexterity tests are available.

Examples of tests of aptitude for specific types of work/jobs
(i) Clerical speed and accuracy

For many lower-level office jobs, especially clerical jobs, an aptitude for identifying, comparing and checking similarities or differences of numerical, verbal or symbolic information is a requirement. This aptitude can also be one requirement of a few higher-level jobs as well, even though it is largely independent of general intelligence. A number of clerical tests are available. There have, of course, been major changes in the nature of office work in recent years. The increased use of electronic equipment in the office of today has been shown to require higher-level checking and coding aptitudes.

(ii) Computer aptitude

Computer programming requires aptitudes to cope with the special forms of logical reasoning required. One tailor-made battery comprising five subtests has been in use for over 25 years and is well validated across many different programming languages. A programming aptitude battery from various other batteries has been developed and validated, with different combinations of tests for different types of programming, systems analysis and software engineering. In addition, the capacity for operating computer hardware is distinct from programming and two batteries have been developed and validated to assess this specific aptitude.

(iii) Language aptitude

The capacity to learn foreign languages is an aptitude that has been identified by research studies. A Modern Languages Aptitude Test may be of interest to organisations that need to train staff to use a number of different foreign languages.

(iv) Sales aptitude

Various tests have been devised specifically to assess the skills required primarily for lower-level sales and sales administration jobs.

Test batteries

At the beginning of this chapter we referred to batteries of tests comprising tests designed to be used together and which cover a wide range of special abilities and aptitudes for specific purposes. Most of these have been referred to in the sections above. For selecting managers and graduates, specific Advanced or Graduate and Management Batteries are available. For apprentices and engineering technicians, various Technical Test Batteries are sold. And there are batteries for office staff.

There are also differential ability batteries that are used widely for selection and that are particularly valuable for counselling purposes. Differential batteries not only provide a score for each specific ability but also present an opportunity to look at the relative scores of an individual across a profile to determine his or her relative strengths and weaknesses. Such batteries can be especially valuable for vocational guidance and counselling, and for placement purposes – allocating a person to a particular job from a choice of many to maximise his or her strengths, and to optimise the job-person match. Individual tests or combinations of tests from the batteries are often used for selection purposes.

Reviews of Level A tests of maximum performance

The British Psychological Society currently publishes detailed technical reviews of 44 tests of the type referred to above that are currently available in the UK. These can be purchased from the BPS Psychological Testing Centre website (www.psychtesting.org.uk). The general aims of this review are:

- to describe the principles of quality control
- to define standards for the evaluation of Level A tests of maximum performance
- to provide fair and balanced evaluations of Level A instruments to help users to judge their suitability for use in occupational assessment.

Ratings are given by two eminent psychologists in the field on a number of attributes similar to those covered earlier in this chapter. Each test is evaluated on: validity, reliability, quality of norms, quality of technical information available, and clarity and coverage of content. We do not have the space to cover 44 instruments here and readers are strongly recommended to refer to the BPS reviews if they wish to consider a range of potential instruments.

PERSONALITY ASSESSMENT AND PSYCHOMETRIC QUESTIONNAIRES

The term 'personality' is all-embracing in terms of an individual's behaviour and the way it is organised and coordinated when he or she interacts with the environment. The sorts of personality characteristics normally assessed include emotional adjustment, social relations, motivation, interests, values and attitudes. However, some psychologists believe cognitive processes (eg intelligence) should also be taken into account when looking at the total personality and so include cognitive scales within their questionnaires. Although psychologists agree that specific aspects of an individual's personality – such as interests, motivations, values and attitudes – are also relevant to occupational assessment and guidance, there are different views on how these aspects relate to one another. Some psychologists see them as overlapping to various degrees with an individual's personality. Others propose a hierarchical model, with personality traits at the bottom, influencing and determining values that in turn influence interests and motivations. These ultimately produce attitudes and a predisposition to behave in certain ways.

Within such a complex and wide-ranging field of study, there are obviously different models and theories of personality. The most recent attempt to summarise the factors measured by the major personality questionnaires has resulted in what has been called the 'big five' model (Barrick and Mount, 1991). Most 'primary' factors are related to one of five 'second-order' factors that can be remembered more easily by the acronym OCEAN:

- Openness to experience
- Conscientiousness

- Extraversion-introversion
- Agreeableness
- Neuroticism-emotional stability.

This model has now gained quite wide acceptance among occupational psychologists although some refer to a 'six-factor' model with motivation separated out from the general Conscientiousness factor.

Self-report personality questionnaires

These are of particular relevance to this book because the large majority of instruments used for occupational assessment of personality, motivations, interests, attitudes and values are self-report questionnaires. Furthermore, as already noted, some are available for use in the UK by non-psychologists provided that they are accredited users (see Chapter 2).

The foundations underlying personality questionnaires are the 'trait' or 'type' theories, which are closely related. The trait approach involves the identification of a number of fairly independent and enduring characteristics of behaviour which all people display, but to differing degrees. An example of such a trait is sociability, with a scale from 'extremely sociable' to 'not sociable at all'. Expressed in its simplest form, what trait theorists such as Cattell and Guilford have done is to identify examples of common behaviour, devise scales to measure these and then obtain ratings on these behaviours by people who know each other well. These observations have then been analysed statistically, using factor analysis, to generate broad traits to be found together but which are fairly independent of other traits.

Groups of traits that are associated, but more loosely, go to make up personality 'types'. Some of the words used to describe traits are also common in everyday language – examples are 'introvert' and 'extravert', 'stable' and 'anxious'. When choosing and using questionnaires, it is important to study the designer's definitions of the traits. Not only may there be important differences between the designer's definitions and those assumed by potential users, but there can also be differences in the way that the same terms have been defined by different designers. Certainly, traits with similar titles can reflect quite different behaviour. Accordingly, the author's definition of a particular trait must always be referred to in order to obtain a clear impression of what behaviour the trait actually represents. For example, the terms 'introversion' and 'extraversion' are used in a different sense in the Myers-Briggs Type Indicator[R] from the way they are used by Cattell, Saville and most other psychologists in this field.

Emotional intelligence questionnaires

This is a domain within personality covering personal characteristics associated with emotional, social and motivational behaviour. Great interest has been shown in recent years in the topic of emotional intelligence (EI), stimulated by a number of books on the subject, and in particular the assertion that EI explains a higher proportion of variance in individual success than IQ. However, there appears from the literature to be some debate about what constitutes the domain of emotional intelligence, about terminology used to describe the construct, and about methods used to measure it.

It has been proposed that high levels of EI are associated with success in a business context, and it is suggested that 'emotionally intelligent' individuals can perceive, understand and regulate the emotions of others, thus making EI a significant factor in the success of interpersonal interaction in a work context. The majority of authors contend that EI elements are personal, not ability, factors, based in part on the results of studies showing clear links between many EI elements and personality factors as measured by personality questionnaires. Emotional intelligence has been defined as 'Being aware of, and managing, one's own feelings and emotions; being sensitive to, and influencing, others; sustaining one's motivation; and balancing one's motivation and drive with intuitive, conscientious and ethical behaviour.'

Currently, there are four different questionnaires available in the UK, all but one of which originate from the USA. They tend to be designed primarily for development applications but can also be used for employment and selection.

Interest questionnaires

These measure broad types of interest in careers and specific types of work activities. They have usually been designed for vocational and career guidance purposes, although most have been used for selection purposes with some positive results. They are designed for use with teenagers and adults.

Values questionnaires

This type of questionnaire covers values such as *interpersonal* ones – support, conformity, recognition, independence, benevolence and leadership – and *personal values* – practical-mindedness, achievement, variety, decisiveness, orderliness and goal-orientation. They tend to be used in the UK more for employment purposes than for counselling.

Work behaviour questionnaires

Questionnaires are available which cover specific work behaviour within the broad personality domain. Two examples quite widely used in the UK are:

- leadership questionnaires, and
- sales aptitude/customer contact questionnaires (see Chapter 12).

Reviews of Level B Questionnaires

Questionnaires have been developed to measure these specific aspects of personality and related characteristics. The choice of which instrument to use depends largely on the nature of the information a user decides is most relevant to his or her purposes and objectives. As with Level A tests, the British Psychological Society currently publishes detailed technical reviews of 60 personality, values, motivation or related questionnaires available in the UK. Reviews can be purchased from the BPS Psychological Testing Centre website (www.psychtesting.org.uk). The general aims of this review are the same as for Level A tests: to describe the principles of quality control, to define standards for the evaluation, and to provide fair and balanced evaluations of these instruments to help users to judge their suitability. Again, ratings are given by two eminent psychologists in the field on the following attributes of each questionnaire: validity, reliability, quality of norms, quality of technical information available, and clarity and coverage of content. Readers are strongly recommended to refer to the BPS reviews if they wish to consider a wide range of potential instruments.

OTHER APPROACHES TO THE ASSESSMENT OF PERSONALITY
Simulation/situational tests

One method of assessing personality that is used quite widely is the use of trained assessors to evaluate clearly defined personality characteristics which are described in behavioural terms so that each assessor is looking for exactly the same qualities (eg assertiveness, flexibility, stress tolerance). Assessors observe the behaviour performance of candidates in situational exercises which simulate work at the level at which candidates will be expected to perform in the organisation. This approach often forms part of an assessment centre, at which candidates are also assessed by other means including interviews and psychological tests. Further details of assessment centres and other methods appear in Chapter 11.

Projective techniques

Each candidate is presented with a relatively unstructured task or with stimuli that provide wide latitude in terms of response. The assumption underlying such methods is that the candidate will 'project' his or her attitudes, values and motivations into responses to the ambiguous material. These methods have sometimes been effective if used alongside an interview by psychologists with special training. They have the specific advantage that they are disguised in their purpose and so it is very difficult for the subject to present a falsely favourable image or desired impression. Techniques such as sentence completion, the Rorschach 'inkblots' and the Thematic Apperception Test (TAT) have been used in personnel assessment with some evidence of success, but they do pose questions about reliability and validity. Furthermore, major problems often arise concerning 'face validity' – ie acceptability to candidates, especially questions of relevance. Projective tests are not available to non-psychologists, and anyone who wishes to try them out is advised to approach only psychologists with extensive experience of their use in the occupational assessment field.

Objective tests of personality

Some psychologists – notably Cattell – have devised experimental laboratory situations to test the hypothesis that psycho-physiological measures – eg heart rate, respiration rate, brain-wave patterns – are correlates of personality characteristics. These tests involve either giving subjects a specific task to perform or subjecting them to some kind of specific stimulus, such as the sound of a gunshot, and measuring changes in psycho-physiological patterns. Although there is limited evidence that, for example, introverts and extraverts behave differently in some of these test situations, the evidence is not strong, and there are major problems in terms of acceptability to subjects! Such methods have not been used in occupational assessment in the UK, although the polygraph (lie-detector), which is a variant of such psycho-physiological assessment methods, has been introduced recently by a few organisations. Its use has, however, been strongly criticised by the British Psychological Society. Again, such methods are beyond the scope of this book.

Fringe methods of personality assessment

The resurgence of interest in scientific personality assessment has also brought in its wake interest in non-scientific methods such as handwriting analysis (graphology), astrology, palmistry, phrenology, and so on. A study by Robertson and Makin (1986) showed that 2.6 per cent of the top 1,000 UK companies always used graphology when assessing managers. This is a relatively low percentage compared with other countries – Schmidt and Hunter (1998) report that 85 per cent of French companies were using graphology in the 1970s, and that in Israel graphology was used more than any other single personality measure.

Yet a major review of the effectiveness of the method by Klimoski and Rafaeli (1983) concluded, in studies that have been scientifically rigorous, that the results have not supported the usefulness of inferences based on handwriting. They concluded that 'given the evidence that we do have, a great reliance on inferences based on script must be considered unwarranted'. Schmidt and Hunter (1998) report evidence that it is not handwriting *per se* that enables limited information to be gathered about personality and job performance, but what people write about! There is also evidence that untrained non-graphologists do just as well (or as badly) as graphologists.

The latest information available about the practice in the UK – the CIPD (2001) survey of test usage – found that 2 per cent of companies still used graphology.

Integrity tests

In recent years, perhaps the most controversial additions to the psychometric armoury have been integrity tests. The Michigan Employability Survey (1989) found that employers were becoming increasingly concerned about the integrity of their employees. Of the 86 employee qualities ranked for importance in entry-level employment, seven of the top eight qualities were related to integrity, trustworthiness and conscientiousness. The majority of research literature that cites the costs of employee theft, fraud and other counterproductive behaviour to organisations comes from the USA. However, it is increasingly clear that UK employers share the same concerns, although they tend to remain very secretive about the methods they use to assess honesty. One indicator of this is that major test producers in the UK are turning their attention to the production of measures relevant to these concerns: the first British example is a questionnaire called Giotto, marketed by the Psychological Corporation.

The term 'integrity' as applied (negatively) within the workplace covers many aspects of employee behaviour – from that which is against civil law (theft, fraud and embezzlement) and against company law (absenteeism, malingering and tardiness) to that which is against the norms of behaviour that are established within a work unit (ie not 'pulling your weight'). Integrity tests are usually differentiated into two general categories of *overt* and *covert* tests (Sackett and Harris, 1984) or alternatively into direct and indirect measures. The distinction between them arises from what the test producers, on the basis of research findings, see to offer strongest predictive power.

On the one hand there is substantial evidence that past behaviour is indicative of future behaviour, as are the attitudes we hold about acceptable behaviour (Cunningham *et al*, 1994). This is reflected in overt integrity test items, which question respondents on their perceptions of

29

specific behaviours in hypothetical situations, as well as directly questioning whether they have committed certain acts of deviance in the past.

On the other hand, covert integrity tests assess certain personality traits of respondents. Research has indicated that there is a very strong relationship between an individual's level of integrity and his or her level of conscientiousness (Ash, 1991). Conscientious employees are hard-working, reliable, dependable and thorough (Murphy and Lee, 1994). As such, they are less likely to engage in counterproductive behaviour, and on the assumption that individuals are more likely to violate work unit norms before civil law, are also less likely to engage in more serious acts of deviance.

Test publishers of overt and covert integrity tests often claim that the tests can accurately predict very specific forms of dishonest behaviour – most commonly theft of cash or stock (Camara and Schneider, 1995). The debate over the extent to which the claims of test producers are met (ie the predictive validity of integrity tests) has raged for a number of years (see Ones *et al*, 1996 for further discussion). In light of the research evidence, the best advice would seem to urge that psychometric measures of integrity should be used with extreme caution – the decision to reject a candidate because he or she poses a high risk of engaging in deviant/dishonest behaviour is a conclusion that should be arrived at on the basis of more than just a score in one test (Baldry and Fletcher, 1997).

Many researchers in this field have suggested the use of weighted application blanks (ie extra weighting being given to certain biographical details that have found to be correlated to an individual's level of integrity), so that very high-risk individuals can be screened out at the beginning of the recruitment process, thereby saving time and money for the organisation and reducing the level of disappointment felt by rejected applicants. Also, there are other, more traditional, assessment techniques that have the potential to contribute to assessing integrity – including references, interviews and simulation exercises (see Fletcher, 1995, for a discussion).

Perhaps most fundamental, though, is the need to keep in mind that integrity and honesty are not completely stable and consistent aspects of an individual's behaviour. Many situational influences, including management practices and ethos, interact with individual predispositions to determine the degree of honesty shown. So achieving high levels of integrity in an organisation is not only (perhaps not even primarily) a selection problem. Integrity is likely to grow and develop in healthy organisations (Newell, 1995) that practise as well as promote it through their HR policies and their attitude to wider aspects of organisational citizenship.

USING TESTS AND QUESTIONNAIRES IN COMBINATION

Tests and questionnaires are often used in combination – for example, the assessment of a top manager may involve reasoning tests, a questionnaire about a cognitive style, a personality questionnaire and a questionnaire about motivation (see Chapter 9). Tests and questionnaires may also be used in combination with other assessment methods such as assessment centres – again details are in Chapter 9.

As a result of their review of 85 years of findings about the validity and utility of selection methods, Schmidt and Hunter (1998) concluded that for hiring employees without experience in the job the most valid predictor of future performance and learning is general mental ability (GMA – ie intelligence or general cognitive ability). In summary, they report a correlation of 0.51. They also found that the three combinations of selection methods which best predicted job performance were GMA plus a work sample test (mean validity of 0.63), GMA plus an integrity test (mean validity of 0.65) and GMA plus a structured interview (mean validity of 0.63).

At first sight these findings provide good evidence in support of testing. However, critics raise several points. First, many of the figures reported are based on mean values, and Schmidt and Hunter actually found that the size of correlation between general mental ability and job performance varied with job level and type – it was 0.58 for professional-managerial jobs, 0.56 for high-level and complex technical jobs, 0.51 for medium technical jobs, 0.40 for semi-skilled jobs, and as low as 0.23 for completely unskilled jobs. Schmidt and Hunter decided to report the summary figure of 0.51 (for medium technical jobs) because this category includes 62 per cent of jobs in the US economy.

Next, it must be remembered that these results are based on follow-up studies published in the research literature. As such they are likely to reflect best practice since research is normally carried out into work that people believe has been done well. In contrast, there is little professional kudos to be gained by the detailed investigation of a selection method which is clearly inappropriate.

Third, critics have pointed out that Schmidt and Hunter's data also shows that people from ethnic minorities are performing less well than whites. Accordingly, some have argued that all the data should be ignored in today's climate in which legislation on both sides of the Atlantic prohibits adverse impact.

Finally, if Schmidt and Hunter's findings are correct, one has to ask why there are so many tests and other selection methods when relatively few might be sufficient. What researchers often do is to try out a battery of existing tests and questionnaires to see if any are effective (as an example, see case study 15, page 77), and only move on to develop new measures if required. However, if and when the research is reported, there may be little or no discussion of the measures that did not work; instead, the paper will be about the 'new' measures that have been successful.

So although Schmidt and Hunter's findings provide useful ideas about tests and other selection methods to consider first in a specific situation, it cannot be assumed that their findings will apply to a particular situation or kind of work. Indeed, years earlier, Ghiselli (1966) had observed and reported the range of correlations found between test results and job performance. These included some negative correlations between test scores and job performance, meaning that the job performance of those with the highest test scores was poorer than the job performance of those with lower scores.

Finally, it should be remembered that this chapter has been concerned with tests and questionnaires. It is rare for a selection procedure to consist only of tests and questionnaires, and it would probably not be good practice. In particular, Schmidt and Hunter found that the best single guide to job performance was work performance tests (mean correlation of 0.54), although of course these cannot be used to select staff without prior experience. Other methods of selection and development are described in Chapter 11.

4

Ethical, legal and social issues

This chapter begins by introducing possible criteria for determining whether or not testing is ethical and then goes on to discuss each criterion in more detail. The criteria are then compared with guidelines from two relevant professional bodies – the British Psychological Society and the Chartered Institute of Personnel and Development.

Next there is an examination of the legal aspects of testing. Finally, there is discussion about social issues associated with the use of tests.

The way that tests are chosen and used can have important implications for those taking the tests, those administering them, existing employees, the local community, and even society as a whole. The impact of testing can range from the success with which individual appointments are made to affecting the image of the organisation as an employer. Some applicants say that they view the care taken with selection as being indicative of the organisation's approach to its people – what some have called the 'employer brand'. In turn this can affect employee satisfaction and, ultimately, commercial and other success.

CRITERIA FOR DETERMINING WHETHER TESTING IS ETHICAL

People who are new to the topic of psychological testing often ask for recommendations about a 'good' test. In a previous chapter we referred to tests that are generally regarded as being 'good' tests insofar as they have been relatively well designed from a technical point of view and have been shown to be effective at measuring what they claim to measure.

However, if testing is to be fully effective from the point of view of both the tester and the person being tested, the technical features of the test are only a part of what has to be considered. In an ideal world it might be argued that a test or tests would be used only under the following circumstances:

- The test has been well designed from a technical point of view. This would include meeting *technical standards* in terms of reliability and validity (see Chapter 2) and being shown to avoid unfair discrimination in terms of sex, race or disability.

- The test is used only in circumstances where its *worth* has been *proved*.

- *Staff* administering, scoring and interpreting the test scores are *specially trained* to appropriate standards. This would include people who work with computers to develop expert systems which 'write' narrative reports based on test scores.

- The *reasons for testing are explained* so that those being tested know why they are being asked to take the tests.

- Those being tested are given *information in advance*, such as a test description handout containing examples of the types of questions and/or practice questions.

- Testing is in accordance with the test designer's recommendations in a *testing environment* that will enable those being tested to give of their best.

- Test results are *scored accurately*.

- Test results are *interpreted accurately*. The need for accuracy now includes interpretation by narrative reports which are generated by feeding test results into computers.

- Records of test results are available to those who have been tested, and they can be given *feedback* about the results and their implications.

- Records of *test scores* and their implications *remain available* to those who have been tested.

- Records of test scores are *used appropriately*.

- All the above processes are *monitored and evaluated* to check their worth and to make improvements where possible.

In practice it would be rare for testing to fully satisfy all twelve conditions listed above. Some of the reasons for falling short of the ideal are detailed below.

Technical standards

One sign of a 'good' test is that it is supported by information about reliability, validity and fairness. However, there are also two potential problems. One is that information about these characteristics is often presented in the form of statistics and many potential test purchasers do not have sufficient understanding of statistics to know what the figures mean. The second is that there are no 'absolute' standards for test design, and acceptability may be a matter of professional or legal interpretation (see Chapters 2 and 7).

Restricting use to situations of proven worth

It might be argued that the use of tests should be confined to specific situations where their worth had been clearly demonstrated. However, at least two potential problems arise. First, the costs of bringing a test to market would be greatly increased if the worth of the test had to be fully proved before it was released, and in practice this would restrict the freedom of choice of test purchasers and users. A particular problem would be to obtain sufficient numbers of people to provide statistically significant evidence from each study. Second, it would mean that use could not be made of the kinds of general trends described by Schmidt and Hunter (1998) who are of the view that procedures do give consistent results across a wide range of circumstances.

This has to be balanced with the view that many factors combine to determine the success of testing in a specific situation including the applicants tested, the work to be done, and the training given. It is unlikely that all these factors will be exactly the same in a new situation.

It is not unknown for tests to be used on a speculative basis – for example, to see whether or not they might give insight into a particular situation, such as understanding why a team of managers appears not to be operating to its full potential. Under these circumstances, feedback is likely to focus on the test or tests that appear to give insight and understanding about the behaviour of the group, rather than tests that do not (see Chapters 2 and 7).

Using specially trained staff

Five levels of training can be identified.

One is the level of training required to administer tests. This involves setting out the room to be used for testing, introducing the tests, and answering any questions raised by those being tested. Accurate timing is important if psychometric tests are to be used properly. The role of the test administrator may also involve marking (but not interpreting) the tests. Some test administrators attend formal training courses, have their skills assessed, and are 'registered' by the course provider; others may be trained 'on the job' by a test user.

A second level is the level of training required to interpret specific tests. People trained to this level will have attended a training course run by a test supplier, and will have been registered by the supplier. Courses of this kind are tending to be replaced by the third level of course.

The third level is the level of training required for the Certificate of Competence in Psychological Testing at Level A. This indicates an understanding of psychometric tests (ie tests of attainment, general intelligence, or special ability or aptitude) to a level which the British Psychological Society considers to be consistent with sound practice.

The fourth and fifth levels refer to the Certificate in Competence in Psychological Testing at Level B for psychometric questionnaires (ie questionnaires measuring personality, interests or values). These certificates are relatively new, and at present only qualified and experienced chartered psychologists have full Level B certificates (ie Level 5). (The certificates of competency are discussed in more detail in the next chapter.)

In practice there is a tendency for people to claim to be trained (when they are not) or for them to claim to be trained to a higher level than is in fact the case. Sometimes the individual is making the claim, but sometimes organisations will ask individuals to do work beyond the scope of their formal training. Sometimes the individual and the organisation conspire to claim a higher level of training than really exists so as to give credibility and/or try to save time or money.

Explaining the reasons for testing

It is reasonable to expect that people who are being tested will be told why they are being asked to take tests and what use will be made of the test results. Research and experience both suggest that some of the most adverse reactions to testing among candidates are caused by lack of information and knowledge about the tests and the way they are being used. To create the right conditions for testing and to ensure that candidates are appropriately briefed, the following steps must be taken:.

- Candidates must understand the place of tests in the selection procedure. This means offering some information on how the tests will be used and on what influence they will have – what weight will be given to them in terms of the whole selection process. Silvester and Brown (1993) found that candidates believed – in the absence of any information – that too much reliance was being placed on test results. Candidates will probably feel more positive if they know that the tests are not normally a pass/fail type of hurdle. Where some of the more common tests are administered, it is perhaps important to indicate that they may be used in different ways (and have different norms) by different organisations.

- Ideally the candidates must be able to see the relevance of the tests to the job requirements. To this end, the tests need face validity (Lounsbury *et al*, 1989; Rynes and Connerly, 1993). In some circumstances this need will have to be weighed against Schmidt and Hunter's view (1998) that a test of general mental ability may be one of the better predictors, but the justification for using such tests comes from the research literature, and until such a test has been trialled there may be no evidence to support its use in a specific situation

- The candidates must be assured of the accuracy or validity of the measures (Rynes and Connerly, 1993) and, by implication, that there is a lack of bias.

- Candidates must be assured of the competence of those using the tests and interpreting the results. A good test can still be rendered worthless by incorrect application or interpretation. Having the BPS Level A and B statements of competence is obviously relevant here. (See also below under *Interpretation*.)

Quite apart from the use of tests in the context of the specific selection procedure, there is the possibility that the results will be referred to later in other situations. For example, within organisations, people who apply for one post and who are unsuccessful may have their test scores and other information passed to other managers. This may be done with the best of intentions, but candidates should nonetheless be assured that their permission will be sought before such information is passed on.

More sinister, in terms of being told the use to which test data will be put, is the practice of inviting individuals to take tests as part of a 'development centre' when the reality is that those who do not reach required standards will find themselves without work and being made redundant. Similarly, some organisations may retain external consultants to administer tests as part of 'career counselling' or 'career development' but may then ask the consultants for reports and use this information to make decisions about the future of those who have been tested.

Giving information in advance of testing

If an individual has had little or no experience of being tested, his or her initial test results may not be accurate. For example, if a reasoning test with a choice of answers is being taken for the first time, the person being tested may be confused by one or more of the features of the test, such as:

- being given a choice of answers and needing to identify the 'correct' one
- being told specifically how to record the answers
- having to strike a balance between working quickly and working accurately. Some people assume that because they have not completed a test of maximum performance, their performance will be judged to be poor – that the majority of applicants for posts are rejected may explain why test results are believed by candidates to have particular influence (see above).

There may also be some confusion among those taking a personality questionnaire for the first time. They may worry excessively about whether they should answer 'Yes' or 'No' to an individual item because they feel they are mainly in the middle, without understanding that any one item will be of very limited significance in terms of the overall scores obtained. Actually, there is quite a strong argument for saying that as part of the information given in advance of testing, some simple background should be provided on how tests are constructed. This helps candidates understand them much better and takes away some of the mistaken beliefs and 'mythology' that surround tests and that can cause apprehension about them.

Information in the form of 'test description handouts' can help people to make appropriate responses. There is evidence that such handouts can additionally play an important part in avoiding unfair discrimination (see below). Guidance to those taking tests is in Appendix III.

The testing environment

So far as psychometric tests are concerned, scores can be maximised by a test environment in which there is an atmosphere of 'quiet urgency'. Lower scores are to be expected in an inappropriate atmosphere (eg one that is too 'laid back' or where there is palpable tension or anxiety) or amid other environmental problems (eg heat, cold, noise, etc).

Accurate scoring

Scoring may be inaccurate for a number of reasons. For example, when psychometric tests are being marked, the wrong answer key may be used (ie the respondents' replies are 'marked' by comparison with incorrect rather than correct answers). Other possibilities are that test scores may be incorrectly totalled, or that errors may be made in transferring an individual's test score onto a summary sheet or other documentation, or into reports. In one episode of the long-running American television series *The Phil Silvers Show*, featuring 'Sergeant Bilko', the sergeant was placed in a platoon for those with high IQs because a golfer stood on the punched card summarising his test scores and the spikes on the golfer's shoe changed his profile for the better.

When optical character readers were used for scoring tests and questionnaires for the first time, rejection and error rates of up to 50 per cent were not uncommon.

Interpretation

Errors can occur in the interpretation of tests and questionnaires. For example, an individual's score on a test (often the number of correct answers) may be compared with the wrong norms – norms are the scores of others who have already taken the test. The same score may look high if compared with a norm group of 16-year-old school-leavers, but low if compared with a group of top managers with business qualifications.

Use of inappropriate norms can also lead to errors in the interpretation of personality questionnaires. There can be other errors, too. For example, in one widely used personality questionnaire, individuals are asked a number of questions about whether they enjoy working with figures. This can sometimes be erroneously interpreted as an indication of *ability* to work with numbers rather than a *preference* for working with numbers – although preference may be affected by ability in the case of some individuals, one does not always correspond with the other: the difference between 'ability' and 'preference' can be really important.

Errors of interpretation may reflect a lack of understanding on the part of the person using the test, or may reflect the way that the results have been expressed in writing. For example, there is sometimes a wish to 'dramatise' the findings in order to make the comparisons between different applicants more vivid. These kinds of errors are not confined to individuals; they can also be found in many computer-generated reports.

Giving feedback

Feedback can be important to people taking tests for a number of reasons. If people are taking tests as part of a selection procedure and are unsuccessful, knowledge of their test results can help them to decide what to do next. For example, if they learn that they reached the required standard but that the vacancy has been offered to an even stronger candidate, they may decide to apply again in the future. If they learn that they are just below the required standard, they may decide to prepare for a future selection procedure and to apply again when they are ready. If they learn that they are well below the required standard, they may decide to stop applying for the same or similar work and to look for alternatives.

However, all these decisions require that feedback is given to the individual, and it is still rare for organisations to give such feedback to all the applicants that are tested.

There is clear evidence (eg Iles and Robertson, 1995; Lounsbury *et al*, 1989) that providing feedback is linked to more favourable attitudes to test use. But perhaps it is not just a question of simply giving feedback – elements of organisational justice theory suggest that it is important for candidates to have the opportunity to correct what they believe are erroneous impressions formed of them. Actually, this seldom happens in the UK because most feedback is provided post-selection decision. In Holland the ethical code for psychologists makes it clear that candidates may require that the results of tests be presented to them before anyone else (de Wolff, 1989).

The availability of records of testing

Records of testing are not always available to the individuals who have been tested after initial decisions have been made. Sometimes the individuals would like to refer back to them. For example, a personality profile may be administered as part of a selection procedure; at a later stage an individual who was tested may ask to see the profile again – if successful, as an aid to thinking about his or her development needs in the new job; if unsuccessful, as an aid to thinking about what to do next.

The appropriate use of records of testing

This relates back to the point made earlier about giving assurances on how test results will be used beyond the situation where they were obtained in the first place. Records of testing may not always be used appropriately. For example, some managers might try to make decisions on the basis of testing that took place months or even years earlier. In the intervening time individuals may have changed considerably, perhaps enhancing their skills or even experiencing a decline in skills because of lack of practice or health or other problems. Although the best tests can provide well-constructed measures of aspects of individuals at a point in time, this does not preclude a degree of subsequent change and development, especially (a) with younger candidates, and (b) in the personality domain.

Monitoring, evaluating and improving

Because of the large number of factors that can affect the success of testing, and the selection and other procedures of which testing may be part, it is important that testing programmes are monitored and evaluated regularly. Later chapters of this book indicate how such reviews may be carried out. However, the statistical and other skills required mean that most readers will need to take professional advice from reputable test suppliers or independent chartered psychologists.

STANDARDS LAID DOWN BY PROFESSIONAL BODIES

Two professional bodies with significant interests in testing are the British Psychological Society (BPS) and the Chartered Institute of Personnel and Development (CIPD).

The British Psychological Society's Steering Committee on Test Standards has published *Psychological Testing – A User's Guide*. The Guide is organised in four sections:

- what to look for in a psychological test
- what qualifies as competence in the use of psychological tests
- a commitment to responsible use of psychological tests
- further information.

In reviewing the responsible use of tests, the Guide identifies the following parties:

- the test developer
- the test supplier

- the test user
- the candidate, the client (who may be one of the above, but may be a third party).

The Guide proposes a set of questions as a means by which each party can contribute to the responsible of psychological tests. Together, the questions and their answers should meet the following requirements:

- that the purpose of testing is clearly stated and communicated to all parties involved in the testing process
- that the procedures for testing are clearly stated and communicated to all parties involved in the testing process
- that it is clear how the test information will be used and communicated to all parties in the testing process
- that procedures for dealing with enquiries and complaints about the process of testing are clearly stated and communicated to all parties involved in the testing process.

The (then) Institute of Personnel and Development published a *Guide on Psychological Testing* in 1997 (IPD, 1997); this replaced the *Code on Occupational Testing* first published in 1988. The Guide aims to ensure that:

- proper consideration is given to the appropriateness of using tests
- tests are used in a professional manner that is relevant to the employment context
- equality of opportunity is ensured throughout the process
- test results are scored, interpreted, evaluated and communicated by appropriately trained individuals
- individuals taking tests are informed of the reasons for the test and the conditions under which it will be used, and how the information will be used and stored, and are given an opportunity to receive feedback on the test results.

Those who wish to avoid bad practice might also find Pickard's 1996 article 'The wrong turns to avoid with tests' helpful.

LEGAL ASPECTS OF TESTING

Current legislation regarding unfair discrimination in the use of tests concerns

- sex discrimination
- racial discrimination
- disability discrimination.

It is virtually inevitable that further legislation will be introduced in the future (eg to avoid unfair discrimination on the grounds of age). In addition, test materials are subject to legislation regarding copyright, while the storage of test scores on computers is subject to the Data Protection Act 1998.

Avoiding unfair discrimination

There are two kinds of discrimination. One, direct discrimination, means that applicants are treated unfavourably because of their sex, their ethnic origin or their disability. The other kind of discrimination, indirect discrimination, is the result of using a selection method that has the consequence of disadvantaging some groups although that may not have been intended. Testing can be a source of indirect discrimination, even though the testing programme may have been introduced with the best of intentions. The unfair discrimination can be caused by the tests themselves, or by the way that the tests are being used.

When choosing tests, the ideal would be for test purchasers to be able to choose from a wide variety of tests which do not discriminate unfairly – but in practice it is very difficult to develop such tests. One reason is that it is generally acknowledged that every individual's environmental and cultural background will affect his or her test performance. The greater the difference between the individual's background and the norm for the culture in which the tests have been developed and used, the greater the possibility of unfair discrimination.

Studies involving the large-scale use of tests have found that many tests show measurable differences in the test scores and profiles of males when compared to those of females and between groups of people of different ethnic backgrounds. These differences can often be shown to be statistically significant. However, statistical significance depends on both the numbers of people in the studies and the size of the difference between the scores of the two groups. Because the numbers of people in the studies are often large, the differences in the scores may be (and often are) small and there is always considerable overlap between the different groups or populations. Debate has therefore centred on four issues:

- First, have 'real ' differences in test scores been found, or could these be the result of errors in sampling or in the choice or use of statistics, etc?

- Second, do any differences that are found reflect differences in the education, experience, opportunity or values of the different groups?

- Third, do any differences found suggest differences between the two groups of a kind that might be related to inherited qualities such as genetic factors?

- Fourth, if differences have been found, can the test be used in a selection procedure if it seems appropriate in other ways?

Whatever the origins of the differences in the test scores, it is often possible to minimise the chances of unfair discrimination when choosing a test. Check the technical manual supplied with the test (all good tests have a technical manual or equivalent document) to see whether the test performance of subgroups (eg men and women, or members of different ethnic groups) has been investigated and reported. If the evidence is available and indicates that the test does not discriminate unfairly, this should be regarded as a positive feature. However, it should not lead to complacency – when using tests, always make arrangements to monitor their use for the possibility of unfair discrimination.

Careful monitoring is particularly important if relevant evidence is not available (as may be the case for a test which is still being developed, or for a few older tests developed before the mid-1970s) or if there is already some unfavourable evidence about a test that is being used because it clearly reflects the requirements of the job and/or has a number of other features in its favour.

Given a situation in which tests may discriminate unfairly, there are several practical points that may make the testing as a whole more acceptable to candidates and that may minimise any unfair discrimination:

- Ensure that both the content of the test and the instructions for completing the test are directly relevant to the vacancies. For example, the use of a test with complex written instructions cannot be justified for a vacancy in which there is little written work to be done – without changes to the instructions, it is likely that the testing would unfairly discriminate against those whose command of written English would be sufficient to do the job.

- Provide test description handouts or example sheets which describe the tests and the reasons for using them, and which give examples of sample questions for the applicants to try. There is evidence to suggest that these approaches have the greatest benefit if applicants are encouraged to do some practice questions rather than simply read about them and/or look at some completed examples. When tests are to be completed against time limits, it can be advantageous to complete the practice examples against time limits too.

- Ensure that the tests being used contain practice examples which the applicants can try immediately before they start the test. Candidates from some ethnic groups or social classes may well be apprehensive when faced with tests – untimed example sessions immediately before testing starts can help to reduce nervousness and unfamiliarity with testing still further, ensuring that when testing starts all the candidates are ready to give of their best.

In the final analysis, tests that discriminate unfairly can be used in selection if they can be shown to predict work performance. Experience suggests that tests which reflect the content of the workplace are less likely to be challenged than those which do not. However, we would hope that progressive employers would not be satisfied with any situation involving discrimination even if their actions were defensible at law. Such employers might be willing to provide alternative entry routes, to place more emphasis on training and less on selection, and so on.

Testing and disability

The Disability Discrimination Act 1995 is accompanied by a code of practice to help employers to comply with their new duties under the Act. The code is not itself law but may be taken into account by a court or tribunal when determining any relevant question. Paragraph 5.12 of the code gives advice on carrying out aptitude and other tests.

The code indicates that aptitude and other tests can be carried out in the recruitment process where the nature and form of the test are necessary to assess a matter relevant to the job. It goes on to give two illustrations of where the use of a test might be called into question:

- The first illustration concerns the use of a numeracy test where the job entails very little numeracy work. It suggests that the requirement for a disabled person to pass the test might be waived.

- The second illustration concerns the use of a short oral test. It is suggested that adjustments might be made (eg giving more time to complete the test, or allowing the test to be taken in written form instead) if oral communication is not relevant to the job.

Both illustrations seem to us to raise the question of why inappropriate tests were being given to applicants (whether disabled or not) more than they afford any profound insight into how to avoid unfair discrimination against disabled people.

Clearly, though, the job analysis has to be scrutinised particularly closely in the context of disability. It is the case that disabled people may tackle a job in a slightly different manner from others, but with equal effectiveness. The need is thus to review what genuinely is essential, rather than just desirable, in terms of the job analysis and person-specification. Nonetheless, if for example a valid selection measure indicates that a person cannot assimilate and use numerical information at a speed that will be necessary to do the job effectively, then the candidate's performance on that measure – whether due to disability or not – can justifiably be used in making the selection decision. Where care has to be taken is in ensuring that performance in selection is going to be typical of performance in the job. Disabled candidates may benefit more than most from being given some practice in dealing with assessment methods that they have not encountered before.

Another issue is the substitution of one assessment method for another to get round the problem posed by a particular disability. For example, if the normal way of assessing achievement orientation is by interview, that could be difficult to apply in the case of a deaf candidate. It may be better to use an appropriate personality questionnaire as an alternative way of getting information on this quality in such a case. Where tests are used, every effort must be made to ascertain the nature and extent of the individual's disability before the testing session, so that suitable arrangements can be made. A few general pointers follow.

- For people with hearing disabilities it will be important to have written test instructions rather than presenting these orally. Communicating starting and stopping times will have to be effected through visual or tactile means. Questions from the candidate about the test can be dealt with either in writing or – if practicable – by sign language.

- For people with visual disabilities, administering tests can represent greater difficulty. In some cases the individual does have a degree of vision and may be able to take tests with the aid of magnifiers or if given large-print versions of the tests. In other cases, Braille versions of tests may be necessary. Increasingly, however, computer-based voice simulation is used by this group. Audio tapes or oral presentation of the test content and candidate responses are other alternatives. At the time of writing, a few of the main test producers have a suite of tests in Braille and/or large-print format; some of these are slightly older versions of the tests currently being marketed. It is important to remember that whatever method is used to assist candidates with reading the tests has also to apply to their use of answer sheets.

It is difficult to specify general advice for people with other disabilities. Candidates with dyslexia will need more time to read the materials, some candidates with motor disorders may find it helpful to have enlarged answer sheets, and so on.

In terms of interpretation, people with disabilities may need longer to complete tests than is normally allowed (and the time required for giving the instructions beforehand may also be greater): this has to be determined on a case-by-case basis. Moreover, their performance on the tests – especially ability measures – cannot be compared in a straightforward way with the standard norm groups, if only because they have frequently taken the tests under slightly different conditions. The small numbers of disabled candidates precludes the development of separate norms for them, so the best advice is to use the normal norm tables, but to interpret them in the light of the likelihood of there being more error in the measurement than is usually the case. The 'true' test score might thus vary more around the score actually obtained to a greater degree than we would expect with other candidates. This means that test scores should be regarded only as approximations, and should be looked at carefully in the context of other assessment data, including the candidate's previous record of achievement.

More detailed advice on testing people with disabilities is outside the scope of this general guide for managers but is available from reputable test suppliers, and an excellent guide is published by at least one of the major test suppliers, the SHL Group.

SOCIAL ISSUES ASSOCIATED WITH THE USE OF TESTS

Elsewhere in this book we have painted a positive picture of the use of tests. At their best they benefit both employers (who are able to identify potentially productive employees) and the employees who are placed in types of work where they can maximise their output and earnings.

Many of the problems that arise from the use of tests are actually a result of the *mis*use of the tests. As psychologists we are disappointed that accounts of the misuse often make reference to 'psychological tests' when the advice of psychologists has either not been taken or has even been ignored.

In theory, individuals can seek redress if they are unfairly adversely affected by testing. However, in practice such actions are stressful for the individual as well as being costly and time-consuming. Individuals may also feel that they will be branded as potential troublemakers, and that no financial award can really compensate for what has been, and what will be, involved.

A particular problem concerns the collection of information about 'suspect' tests – ie those tests for which there is little or no evidence of technical worth. It could be argued that it would be helpful for British law to be changed to accommodate 'group actions'. The work of a chartered psychologist could then form part of legal action taken on behalf of a large number of people who felt that they had been treated unfairly by the use of a test, rather than focusing on a particular use of a test by a single employer.

There remains the issue of the impact of tests even if they were used according to best ethical practice. Would we then have some kind of Utopian situation at work? Our views are that:

- tests will always have limitations
- different opinions will remain
- wider social issues have to be considered.

The limitations of testing

Individual performance at work always has a number of elements. Even for relatively straightforward jobs there are a number of elements, such as the quality and quantity of output, ease or difficulty of supervision, relationships at work, timekeeping and attendance. For more complex jobs there are issues such as strategic thinking, relationships with customers, organisational skills, efficiency and effectiveness. In addition, there are issues for all employees around motivation and ambition. It is rare for an individual employee to be consistently good (or consistently poor) at all features of his or her work – rather, people tend to perform well in some areas and less well in others.

Individual tests cannot be expected to predict all elements of performance. Accordingly, they should never be used for selection on their own, and even combinations of tests have limitations in predicting all aspects of performance at work. Arguably the best indicator of performance at work is a sample of performance of work (eg performance during a trial period), but even this has limitations because people differ in their ability and interest in developing to meet future job requirements. Indeed, Schmidt and Hunter (1998) say that in their experience supervisors are reluctant to terminate poor performers because doing so is an unpleasant experience for them.

Different opinions

At the end of an assessment procedure involving the use of tests, most candidates are perceived to have some positive features, and most have some negative features too. In spite of careful preparation and agreement about what is to be assessed and why, there can be differences of opinion about the importance of differences in test scores, the relative importance of different tests and other information.

Particular debate may centre on the differences in style that can be accommodated in a particular role, and the extent to which an individual may be able to adapt. For example, one successful strategic director in a large organisation became 'stuck' at its lower levels because his somewhat cerebral approach was seen to be far better suited to strategic headquarters than to the operational side of the business. Yet he himself realised that without the operational experience his future career would be severely limited. He obtained the operational experience that he required at his thirteenth attempt.

In general, assessment procedures do seem to be helping some people to identify their strongest abilities and to put them to good use early in their careers. However, they may be less successful in helping people to leave behind their proven skills and abilities and to take on responsibilities in new areas. People may thus feel trapped in areas of work in which they are proficient but increasingly bored.

Wider social issues

Throughout this chapter we have repeated that in the eyes of the law, unfair discrimination is avoided if the contents of tests reflect the content of work to be done. This means that tests are likely to become more, rather than less, job-related. In turn, those who can learn about the content of the work to be done in advance of the selection procedure are likely to do better than those who are unable to do so.

Unless those responsible for testing make fairness a priority, testing may favour the better educated and the better informed. For example, ability tests that are administered by computer may be completed better by those familiar with computers (because they or their school could afford them) than those who have little or no prior experience.

Some may be content that this is the case, and that investment in education and individual study and effort are being rewarded. Others may wish to reflect on the experiences of the British Army in the middle of World War II, when there was a complete lack of confidence in the process for identifying officers.

Before this time, potential officers had been selected by a short interview. Toplis and Stewart (1983) describe details given in a 1942 edition of the magazine *Picture Post*:

> *A man who showed promise in his unit was recommended to the CO [commanding officer] for interview. On the strength of the interviewer's impression in a 15-minute talk, the candidate was either rejected or sent on a course at the OCTU (officer cadet training unit). Stories got around that it was no good putting up for commission unless you'd won your colours at cricket and rode to hounds.*

> *For this reason, the numbers wanting to be officers had virtually dried up in the middle of war. Worse still, half the candidates recommended for commission proved unsuitable to become officers when tested in actual training. Alarmed Members of Parliament learned what was happening and asked questions in the House of Commons.*

A new approach to selection was taken when War Office Selection Boards were set up. Garforth, a professional soldier, described the methods used:

> *Tests may vary from a 'group discussion', in which eight or ten candidates sit round in easy chairs and are told to select a subject for discussion and talk about it to each other, to a 'group task' which may involve improvising, with limited materials found on the spot, some method of 'escaping' as a group over a wire entanglement, including electrified wire and alarms. In another form of the test, groups are told to invent their own situations and act on them.*

These methods were added to other methods of selection (such as individual interviews, intelligence and other tests, and medical examinations) to assess the subject's ability to get on with, and influence, his colleagues, to display qualities of spontaneous leadership and to think and produce ideas in a real-life situation.

The *Picture Post* article reported that since the new boards had been set up, the numbers of men applying for commissions had doubled. After the war the general approach of the boards was copied by the British Civil Service and by commercial organisations on both sides of the Atlantic.

Testing and other selection methods do not have to favour the better educated and better informed – whether they do so is currently a matter for the designers of selection methods and the employers who use them. Ultimately, the government must decide whether legislation is required.

Future legislation

It is possible that future UK or European legislation will affect testing. Some possibilities are examined in Chapter 12.

5
Obtaining tests

As mentioned in Chapters 1 and 2, properly designed psychological tests and questionnaires are supplied only to people who have appropriate training. Accordingly, managers or others who wish to introduce tests or widen the range of tests being used have to consider how it might best be done. In practice, there are four traditional ways of doing it.

The first is to have existing staff (such as HR managers) obtain a Certificate of Competence in Occupational Testing, awarded after attendance on a recognised course run by test suppliers or chartered occupational psychologists. A second option is to recruit an individual who already possesses the Certificate of Competence. The other two options involve employing a chartered occupational psychologist either as a consultant or as an internal adviser.

Each option is discussed in turn.

Three other issues are then raised. First, some readers may be keen to know more about tests which can be administered over the Internet. Second, some may be tempted to use the Internet as a source of test supply. Finally, there is a warning about the 'Barnum effect' first mooted in Chapter 1.

TRAINING COURSES

People who want to use tests or questionnaires to assess others should successfully complete an appropriate course (or courses) run by a chartered occupational psychologist. To start, they should attend a Level A course that covers ability and aptitude tests, as well as the basic principles and practice of test administration, scoring and interpretation. Those who wish to go on to use Level B questionnaires (such as personality and interest inventories) must attend a further training course geared to the specific questionnaires that they wish to use. An assessment of the likely worth of specific tests should therefore be made before attending a training course. Information about the possible benefits of using the test can be obtained from the training course organisers or from the suppliers of the tests featured in the training courses. Note that courses run by test publishers are usually confined to their own tests, whereas non-publisher trainers often draw on tests from a number of publishers.

It is important that those sent for training possess the qualities that will enable them to administer, score, interpret and defend the appropriate introduction and use of tests. A good level of intelligence is also required in order to understand the principles involved and to explain them to others. Specific aptitudes are also required to deliver test instructions, mark tests quickly and accurately, interpret scores and explain the results to others both orally and in writing. Finally, competence in the use of PCs is also of value. The demands made by Level B training courses are greater than those made by Level A.

In addition to being able to understand the contents of the training courses, successful users ideally need two other qualities. First, they must have a good understanding of the world of work, particularly the different management and other functions and the similarities and differences between them. Second, they must have an understanding of the range of abilities and behaviours among people at work, and the causes of satisfaction and dissatisfaction at work.

The cost of training can be considerable, covering tuition fees, residential fees and travel. In addition, there is the 'opportunity cost' of absence from work and the cost of obtaining supplies of testing materials. For example, at the end of 2003, one leading test publisher was charging £1,915 + VAT for a five-day non-residential course leading to a Level A certificate (£2,285 for the equivalent residential course). Those with a Level A certificate could register for a five-plus-one-day course leading to a Level B intermediate certificate – the costs were £2,250 + VAT (non-residential) and £2,610 + VAT (residential).

Once a member of staff is trained, the cost for that person to run a testing programme may be low compared with the other options of regularly involving consultants or employing specialist internal staff, although some test suppliers require registration or licence fees and there is the cost of the test materials too. For example, one of us uses a combination of tests and questionnaires to advise on top and senior appointments. At the time of writing (April 2004) the cost of these test materials was around £50 for each candidate. In addition, an annual licence fee of £500 + VAT is payable to one test supplier whereas another aims to make it a condition of supply that people return for refresher training and updating every three years. Note that these short training courses cannot give people the considerable expertise required to develop or evaluate sophisticated testing systems, and an occupational psychologist should be retained to do this (see below).

Once an organisation has one or more staff with the requisite training, it may be sensible to train less senior staff to carry out the actual test administration. Training can be given by those holding the BPS Certificate or by attending a course for administrators run by the test suppliers. Details of Level A and B courses to be run during the subsequent two months appear in the BPS journal *Selection and Development Review* (SDR), published bi-monthly.

BPS Certificates of Competence

In response to earlier concerns about the widespread misuse of tests within many organisations, the BPS established a set of Standards in Occupational Testing in order:

- to ensure that its members, and other test users, act in a professional manner, and to agreed minimum standards
- to provide a means for recognising users who are competent, and
- to establish minimum standards for training in the use of psychological tests.

The certification scheme provides an agreed set of standards relating to the fair and effective use of tests, and requiring certificate holders to adhere to a code of practice and professional conduct defined by the BPS and supported by the CIPD. The standards have been designed to fulfil a number of functions, including the provision of criteria to be used for assessing competence and for issuing guidance to those who may wish to employ testers.

The standards of competence for Level A cover the following areas:

- relevant underpinning knowledge, especially the nature and the theory of testing

- task skills such as test administration and giving feedback to candidates and clients

- task management skills relating to, for example, organising procedures and materials

- contingency management skills covering, for example, problems, difficulties and breakdowns in routine

- contextual skills relating to the appropriate integration of testing to other parts of the job role – ie when to use tests and when not to

- instrumental skills relating to a general knowledge of types of test, different modes of delivery, and knowledge of the tests used.

Some Level A courses run by chartered occupational psychologists are advertised as 'providing training leading to fulfilment of requirements for the BPS Certificate of Competence in Occupational Testing at Level A', and so obviously provide automatic qualification. Other Level A courses 'provide training leading to partial fulfilment of the requirements ...', so that further verification of testing work is required before the certificate is awarded, subject to acceptable performance.

The BPS currently charges £50 for awarding the certificate and an annual fee of £20 for inclusion on the register. It encourages test publishers to supply relevant tests only to people who hold the certificate, and employing organisations to use only such staff for testing. Another benefit for members is a free subscription to *SDR*, which normally costs £37 per annum. Furthermore, as noted in Chapter 2, the BPS now runs its own Psychological Testing Centre which produces reviews of most of the widely used tests and questionnaires.

The Level B standards apply to those who wish to use tests of habitual or typical performance – eg personality, interests, motivation, values and attitudes. Certificates are awarded only to those qualified at Level A and who have demonstrated competence in using Level B tests. These standards cover a number of units grouped under three broad aspects of competence: foundation knowledge, test use, and test choice and evaluation. Through the accumulation of relevant units, people can obtain either an intermediate Level B certificate (competent in the administration and interpretation of one instrument) or a full certificate (competent in two or more). Upgrading is possible, and no further fee is required for Level B membership. As with Level A, some courses at Level B lead to a Level B intermediate certificate, whereas others require additional work and verification.

For information on course providers, readers are advised to visit the BPS website given below, or contact the test suppliers, many of which are listed in Appendix I or in *Selection and*

Development Review. Full information about the requirements for both Level A and B is available from the BPS PCT website (www:psychtesting.org.uk).

Since 1991, a total of 17,495 people have obtained the Level A certificate, some 1,200 to 1,500 obtaining the certificate in most years. Since 1996, 4,606 have obtained the Level B intermediate certificate, 400 to 700 obtaining the certificate in most years. Just 62 people have obtained the full Level B certificate.

RECRUITING CERTIFICATED STAFF

It may be appropriate to recruit staff who hold a certificate of competence in occupational testing, particularly when the use of tests forms part of the job description for the vacancy to be filled. The BPS holds a register of those who hold the certificates and can thus verify any claims made. It may be appropriate to take some account of the particular tests that individual applicants can order without attendance on additional familiarisation courses. More important, it is sensible to find out which Level B tests each applicant is already registered to use, because these tests are still supplied by individual publishers, and additional training in the use of a specific questionnaire means additional time and cost even if a Level B certificate is already held.

RETAINING AN INDEPENDENT CONSULTANT

An independent consultant may be of help in several ways. First, if tests are not already in use, advice can be taken on whether there may be financial or other advantages to be gained through their introduction. In making such a review, account must be taken of the types of test that might be used, and whether or not the organisation's own staff should be trained to use them.

Second, if tests are already in use, the consultant's advice may be helpful in determining whether or not the tests are effective and fair, either individually or in combination. In addition, the consultant can advise on the likely benefits of introducing different tests, designing tailor-made tests, etc. The design of tests for specific situations can be an attractive strategy if large numbers are to be tested and/or the qualities to be tested are beyond the normal range of tests. It may also be relevant to review other stages of the recruitment and selection procedure.

Third, some occupational psychologists work in professional groups and can thus offer a range and depth of specialisms. Between them the group members may be able to access a wide range of tests, offer statistical and other support, arrange in-house training courses, etc. Suitable consultant occupational psychologists can best be identified by reference to the register of chartered occupational psychologists published by the British Psychological Society and to the Society's register of those who hold the certificate of competence in occupational testing. Psychologists who have an interest either in the sales of particular tests or in running training courses in testing should obviously disclose their interest in preliminary discussions.

Advice on testing is sometimes offered by consultants and others who are not psychologists, often on the basis of holding one or more certificates of competence in occupational testing. Some may have considerable and sound relevant experience, but others may have gained little practical or other experience since gaining the certificate. Remember that it is only chartered psychologists who can design and run training courses for non-psychologists, and who are obliged to follow the standards relating to the use of tests drawn up by the British Psychological Society.

EMPLOYING SPECIALIST STAFF

The fourth possibility is for an organisation to consider the appointment of its own occupational psychologist. This again should ensure an impartial assessment of the potential benefits of testing and other assessment methods. However, the commitment to employ an occupational psychologist on anything other than a short-term contract would be making assumptions about the value of using tests and about the level of recruitment in the months and years ahead. Although the psychologist might be able to contribute to many other aspects of the organisation besides selection, the short-term and long-term role of the psychologist would have to be fully considered before this option was chosen.

Such a strategy is most appropriate when there is scope for large-scale testing and assessment and when considerable savings can be made by developing in-house tests and training courses tailor-made to the organisation's needs. Although many major UK organisations now employ their own occupational psychologists, some have appointed a relatively junior and inexperienced person as their in-house psychologist and have not been happy with the advice given. All in all, if there is a sufficient volume of work, there may be advantages in seeking advice from an independent occupational psychologist initially, and then evaluating the other options in the light of experience of the benefits of testing and other skills experienced at first hand.

TESTING VIA THE INTERNET

Traditional tests were in a pencil-and-paper format. However, during the last few years there has been a dramatic increase in other media for administration – first answer sheets that could be computer-scored, then tests that could be administered on personal computers, and now tests that can be administered over the Internet. Indeed, no other single factor has had such a major impact on the 'testing industry' over the last 100 years than this. If you search on the Internet for a personality-type questionnaire, you will find literally hundreds of different versions, the vast majority of which are not psychometric tests – they are really 'quizzes': simply lists of questions. But reputable test publishers are beginning also to put their wares on the Internet. This is not surprising, however, in the light of the large number of potential benefits that, it is claimed, the Internet can provide for both users and publishers. In addition, there seems to be a high demand for Internet testing among HR professionals. *People Management* (2001b) conducted a survey and found that 'more than three quarters of the HR professionals want the [online testing] service'. All the same, 30 per cent of them did have reservations – they did not want it yet, mainly because current packages did not give them sufficient control over the testing environment.

Advocates of Internet testing put forward a number of important advantages. One of the main potential benefits of Internet testing is access to test users and takers world-wide. Anyone with a PC linked to the Internet can sit a test, the results can be processed almost instantly, and a report can be produced and sent to users or test-takers within a few minutes. The publishers can then use the data for conducting further development work and research on their instruments in order to improve them and demonstrate their effectiveness. Test results can be used by companies for screening applicants for jobs in order to reduce large applicant pools quickly and effectively. In addition, the Internet could also significantly increase the number of people who take tests for self-development purposes and dramatically reduce the costs. These are just a few of the potential benefits claimed by advocates of Internet testing.

Many concerns about general testing practices described so far in this book are also relevant to Internet testing. One major concern is that testing should be conducted under highly controlled conditions and like ability tests should be timed to the nearest second. Although timing can be controlled by the computer program, the general testing environment cannot. Such controls are difficult to achieve remotely. Significant questions are also raised about confidentiality of test results and reports, and about who should have access to the data. Furthermore, how can the layperson decide if a test on the web is a reputable psychometric instrument or a 'Mickey Mouse quiz'?

But the question most difficult to answer and resolve is: How do you know who is responding to the test at the end of the line? If the test is being used for selection, many would be tempted to ask, and perhaps pay, someone who they know is a genius to take the test for them. Although sophisticated recognition systems have been invented, using fingerprints or the retina of the eye, it would still be necessary to have the correct original against which to compare the specimen presented by the test-taker.

Finally, there are a number of technical matters yet to be fully resolved, many of which relate to compatibility of different operating systems and software. If the system is not well-nigh perfectly reliable, it could make ability testing under strict time conditions rather risky. If the system breaks down mid-way, one cannot ask the person to start again, because of practice effects.

In an article on Internet testing, Professor Dave Bartram (2001), President of the International Test Commission and R&D Director of SHL, reported that his company had launched its first web-based service one year earlier, and that clients were already seeing benefits in terms of time and cost of recruitment. However, he acknowledged many of the problems of Internet testing and proposed that 'testing on the Internet can take place under three main conditions':

- uncontrolled (no training or accreditation required) and unsupervised – the test-taker merely registers on the open Internet

- controlled but unsupervised, in which the user registers the candidate, definitively verifying his or her identity, but otherwise does not supervise the testing

- controlled and supervised, in which a qualified test user conducts all aspects exactly as in a face-to-face situation.

Tests carried out under each condition would have different classifications for use. Professor Bartram also noted that

The International Test Commission is considering a classification and accreditation scheme that all publishers could adopt and that would provide an indication of the qualities of an instrument (for

example, have its psychometric properties been evaluated, or is it only a set of questions?) and the conditions under which it has been designed to be used.

Irrespective of whether a test is administered by traditional means or via the Internet, there remains a strong requirement to assess the providers and their products.

CHECKING OUT TESTS FROM OTHER SOURCES

Because of the cost of obtaining reputable psychological tests, some managers may be tempted to try some of the materials available from non-psychologists, especially on the Internet, which are claimed to measure ability, personality, etc. Although such materials are often well presented, there is seldom any technical information of the kind described in Chapter 2 to back up claims about the value of the techniques. If these or other instruments are used, there is the danger not only that they may select the wrong people but that their use could not be justified at an employment tribunal and that the reputation of the employing organisation could be severely damaged. Mention has already been made of the fact that some tests that fail to meet psychometric standards have appealing graphic design, and those contemplating the use of tests must be careful not to base their judgements on appearances alone.

There are two other reasons why some unproven tests may be widely used. The first is that some managers lack the kind of information available in this book and do not appreciate the kind of information that should be available about a test. The second reason is the widespread use of a 'ploy' to sell measures purporting to assess personality. The ploy involves asking managers to complete a questionnaire and subsequently discussing their results with them. The results can seem quite impressive – a powerful and personal demonstration of validity. Unfortunately, it is no such thing.

This was nicely demonstrated in a classic study by Stagner (1958) who gave a personality inventory to a group of 68 personnel managers at a conference, then took their papers away for scoring. Later, the participants were given a report describing their personality as shown by their results. Fifty per cent rated their report as 'amazingly accurate', 40 per cent as 'rather good', and the remaining 10 per cent judged it as 'about half and half'. None rated their reports as 'more wrong than right' or as 'almost entirely wrong'. It was then revealed to the managers involved that they had in fact all been given exactly the same personality description, which was nothing to do with the personality inventory. How could the participants have been so convinced yet so deceived? But they are not alone. This study has been repeated many times and the same results found, even when the participants have been given reports containing unflattering descriptions of themselves.

The phenomenon is called 'the Barnum effect', after the showman of that name. It is in effect a trick. The personality descriptions are loaded with vague generalities which are actually applicable to most people – statements like 'I am sometimes not as confident as I appear.' Not surprisingly, when faced with a whole series of such truisms presented by a consultant or other 'expert' as being the product of a carefully constructed test, people tend to be impressed. After all, what they are being given is for the most part correct as far as it goes – the trouble is, it does not differentiate one person from another, and it is unlikely to be of any use in decision-making.

Something similar happens when you visit a fortune-teller ('I see a tall, dark stranger . . .') or when graphologists 'prove' that handwriting analysis is the key to personality assessment by giving a description based on somebody's signature. Although it often goes against the grain to admit it, judging the worth of a personality measure on the basis of one's perceptions of its accuracy in describing oneself is woefully inadequate.

Tests developed outside the UK

Test materials developed in the USA and overseas sometimes have good technical information but could require substantial adaptation before they could be used with confidence in the UK. A qualified occupational psychologist with appropriate knowledge and experience should be retained to make this adaptation.

6

Testing strategies

A reader who is thinking of using tests for the first time may be puzzled by the position of this chapter in the book. Having just written about how to obtain tests, the next issue to address would seem to be how to choose a test for a specific purpose. However, testing a testing strategy for an organisation, for a group or even for an individual must be considered, for three reasons.

First, even if tests are going to be used only for selection purposes, there are two questions:

- Which test or tests are going to be for which procedures?
- At which stage in the procedures are the tests going to be used?

Second, tests and questionnaires can be used not only for selection but for other purposes including personal development, individual counselling, and team-building. From the point of view of the test-takers it is normal to limit the use of individual tests or questionnaires to particular situations. If this is not done, some people in an organisation might be given a reasoning test to help them to formulate a personal development plan and then might be asked to take the same test a few days later as a part of an assessment for promotion. Retaking a test in this way is likely to favour the individuals concerned and to give them an unfair advantage over any other applicants.

Finally, account must also be taken of the implications of any strategy in terms of the need to train HR and other staff to use the specific tests.

This chapter on testing strategies therefore covers:

- agreeing the main reason for testing – eg (i) as part of a selection procedure, or (ii) for development or other purposes
- how the tests will be administered
- whether internal and external applicants are to be treated in the same way
- testing overseas
- anticipating all the consequences.

AGREEING THE MAIN REASON FOR TESTING

Organisations often start to develop their testing strategy by deciding which tests and/or questionnaires are going to be used for selection. Because selection may involve people already working in the organisation ('internal' candidates) as well as people who would be new to the organisation ('external' candidates), the tests must be kept secure and restricted to use in selection – in fairness to the external candidates they should not be for other purposes such as training or the development of existing staff, thus giving internal candidates an unfair advantage.

In addition, the tests chosen for selection should meet a series of technical criteria and their availability will be restricted (see Chapters 2 and 7) – there would be no point in using a selection method which potential applicants could access on the Internet or in other ways (see case study 8, page 5).

This leads on to a further point – about whether external applicants who are rejected should be allowed to attempt a test on a second occasion – and if so, what the time interval should be. One view on this is that applicants who meet the other selection criteria should be allowed a second attempt after three months (on the grounds that the first score or profile may not have yielded a 'true' score or profile, and/or that the individual may have done suitable training or development in the intervening period). However, if the applicant does not meet the requirement on the second occasion, the interval before taking the test again might be increased to 12 months to avoid a situation in which a candidate could take a test of questionnaire repeatedly until he or she 'passed' as a result of trial and error!

Once it has been agreed which tests are to be used for selection purposes, decisions about which tests to use for development can be made from among the many remaining tests – indeed, some tests and questionnaires have been designed for use in development activities rather than for selection.

Testing as part of a selection procedure

Tests can be given:

- as an aid to short-listing
- as part of the main selection procedure
- as part of a detailed check on the final few candidates.

Tests as an aid to short-listing

Imagine a situation in which reasoning tests are being used as part of a time-consuming selection procedure in which a large proportion of the applicants are failing to reach the minimum standards required on the tests. If there is good reason to believe that performance on these tests will be a valid predictor of subsequent job performance and that they will not discriminate unfairly (two key criteria for choosing tests for use at any stage of a selection procedure), there may be considerable savings in time and effort by using the tests at an earlier stage in the selection process as a method of sifting.

For example, the first stage in a revised approach to selection might be for applicants to complete an application form. The second stage might comprise a systematic sift of the forms combined with a short interview, possibly on the telephone, with the more promising candidates. The third stage might entail calling a group of the more promising candidates in (a) to give them information about the organisation and the particular vacancies, (b) to administer tests, and (c) to give brief interviews concerning key issues or requirements. As a result of this preliminary work, the success rate among those invited back to the time-consuming selection procedure is likely to rise to an acceptable level.

It may be possible to make even bigger savings through 'streamlining' the testing arrangements by, for example, administering tests over the Internet. This is now common for graduate recruitment. However, a more traditional example is where applicants are brought to a central point to be tested in large groups by pencil-and-paper tests and in this way the cost of the administrator's time could be minimised. Normally a single administrator can test about 20 people (for larger groups assistance is required). Further savings can be made by using special answer sheets that can be scored quickly using carbon paper or scanned into a computer for scoring. Major employers dealing with very large numbers may find it worthwhile to have tests administered on PCs so that scoring and report-writing can be done automatically (see Chapter 11).

Sifting procedures of this kind are in fact operated by major employers who receive large numbers of applications. Each year large organisations receive several thousand applications from graduates seeking a career in management, and the decision on which applicant to call to the main selection procedures (which may be an assessment centre lasting 24 hours) is partly based on the result of job-related tests. A more radical sift has been carried out in recent years by the Civil Service Commission who had been faced with up to 10,000 applicants for as few as 200 vacancies for their top posts. Tests were used to reduce the number of candidates by 80 per cent or more, but many occupational psychologists would regard this high level of dependence on tests as contentious.

However, four points have to be made about the use of tests as a means of short-listing. The first is that when tests are used as a way of reducing large numbers, there is often a temptation to control the number of applicants invited to the final selection by the simple method of raising or lowering the 'cut-off' or 'pass' mark without thinking through all the possible consequences. There are real dangers in this kind of *ad hoc* approach – if those with low marks are 'passed', they may be found to lack the abilities required to do the job, whereas restriction to those with only the highest marks may eliminate candidates with a wide range of other strengths. This issue is examined in more detail in Chapter 8.

Second, tests are not the only method of short-listing. Others include short-listing on the basis of replies on standard or supplementary application forms. Some organisations use 'bio-data', an approach in which numerical values are assigned to candidates' biographical replies according to research based on past applicants. For internal candidates, supervisors' reports can be another factor to take into account.

A third point about short-listing is that there is sometimes scope for reducing numbers by giving more opportunity for self-selection: in this way, the cost of testing and interviewing people who eventually decide they do not want the job can be avoided. So while it is the normal aim of an advertisement to attract as many applicants as possible, an advertisement for a job that is likely to be popular might also contain information about some of the less appealing aspects of the work – for example, the need to spend a lot of time away from home, or to be on call to deal with emergencies, or to work in difficult or unpleasant conditions.

When organising and running selection procedures it is possible to calculate, or at least estimate, the ratios between the numbers attending the final selection procedure, the numbers offered appointments, the numbers accepting, and the numbers actually starting. Short-listing or self-selection requires an excess of applicants over the numbers that are to be called to the subsequent stages in the selection procedure. If there is no such excess, there is a conflict between the use of short-listing methods on the one hand and filling all the vacancies on the other. Under these circumstances there is a range of possible management strategies ranging from readvertising to reviewing and adjusting the nature of the work, the training offered and the working conditions to make the work more attractive to applicants.

Tests as part of the main selection procedure

There are several reasons why it could be desirable for tests to form part of the main selection procedure rather than be a separate part. First, separate testing may be considered unacceptable by candidates. This might be true if, for example, considerable travel was to be involved so that applicants might require a day's absence to attend testing and a further day to attend for interview.

A second reason for testing as part of the final procedure is that the results can then be used in taking stock of both the strengths and weaknesses of each candidate. However, if this is done, then some difficult decisions may have to be faced. For example, a candidate with a number of past achievements may have a single indifferent test score and his or her potential for work at a higher level may therefore be questioned. Because test scores can sometimes be very good guides to potential, it can be difficult to make the 'right' decision. Clearly, a decision based on evidence from follow-up studies of past selections would be preferable to an *ad hoc* decision (see Chapter 8).

A third reason for testing being part of the final selection procedure could be to allow all internal candidates the opportunity to take part in the full assessment and thus to confirm an organisation's interest in the development of its own staff whenever possible.

Tests as part of a detailed check on the final few candidates

Some organisations use tests as part of a final check on applicants rather than in a preliminary sift. There can be several reasons for this, including the fact that the final assessors may be senior staff from a head office or other location who have access to tests that are not available locally. Sometimes consultant occupational psychologists (from within or outside the organisation) are asked to advise at this late stage of selection and to use tests as part of final procedures. This strategy is of particular use when those involved in the earlier stages of selection are not accredited test users, when the most appropriate tests are available only to the psychologists, and/or when a view is required of how applicants compare with standards outside a particular organisation. The individual assessment of candidates may also be preferred when there is a need for security about the vacancies and/or the individual applicants.

A final reason for delaying the involvement of experts until the end of the procedure is the view that their in-depth and sometimes expensive assessments should be confined to the most promising candidates only (see Chapter 8).

Testing for development and other purposes

Tests can be used not only for selection but also as an aid to helping employees with their career development. Tests can be used to help gauge suitability for specific vacancies or training opportunities (such as computer programming), or can be used as part of a process of helping individuals plan their career development by providing them with objective feedback about their abilities, aptitudes, personality, values and interests.

There are two main ways in which tests can be used as an aid to career development. First, they can be used by an occupational psychologist or suitably qualified HR manager working with just one individual. The individual being counselled may agree to take a variety of tests and questionnaires and may then be counselled about the results and the implications. Such work can be demanding on the individual counsellor, who has to have an appreciable breadth and depth of knowledge about tests and occupational information both within and outside the organisation. However, such counselling can be carried out in confidence and at relatively short notice.

CASE STUDY 10

Advice on career choice

After leaving college, a man in his early 20s started work in a property agency. In the first year he worked hard and was given a good annual appraisal. In his second year he worked even harder but his annual appraisal indicated that he had had only an average year. In the third year he redoubled his efforts, only to be told at the end of the year that he should be considering his future. Bewildered, he sought advice from his father, who in turn asked for advice from one of the authors.

At interview, the son explained that he was the first to arrive in the office and the last to leave. His files were always neat and tidy and he always returned telephone calls promptly. In contrast, his colleagues arrived late, had long lunches, and worked from untidy desks covered with papers.

A personality questionnaire confirmed the picture emerging from the interview. The son was someone who seldom had original ideas, who tended to pay attention to detail, and who tended to be very respectful of others. In contrast, the property agency wanted people with originality who could elbow their way into profitable business deals – only essential details really mattered. The son is now working happily and successfully for a different employer with conservative values and more traditional ways of doing business.

A second approach to career development that may involve tests is the assessment centre (see Woodruffe, 2000, and Chapter 11 below). Initially, such centres were another form of selection, attempting to assess those individuals who had the attributes identified as being important in long-term managerial success (Dulewicz, 1991). In time, however, the emphasis has changed and many assessment centres are now much more oriented towards helping individuals to achieve greater awareness of their own strengths and weaknesses and subsequently using this information for planning their development. Accordingly they are sometimes called 'development centres', 'development workshops', etc.

Such centres can require careful preparation – for example, a number of existing jobs may have to be analysed in order to identify the underlying competencies, while credible but independent assessors have to be identified and trained. Bearing in mind that they may be attended by numbers of key staff, centres must also be scheduled for times that will not disrupt the organisation as a whole. All in all, such centres tend to be more complex both technically and administratively and can be very difficult to arrange at short notice.

At the development centres, participants are often required to work together and/or compete against each other, so that they may have the opportunity to assess their own performance against that of the other participants. Because such centres often involve key HR and other managers with contrasting backgrounds and experience as assessors, there can be a wide and informed view of opportunities within the organisation. Above all, the information obtained about the participants is relatively objective and in this way compares favourably with the information based on rumour, reputation and mutual admiration on which some senior appointments can be based.

Psychological tests may be used as part of a development centre, just as they might be used as part of an assessment centre for selection. Further tests are widely used as a way of selecting which people might attend an assessment or development centre. This reflects the fact that such centres are expensive and not everyone will benefit from attending, and so it makes sense both for individuals and organisations to try to ensure that only those who will get something from the experience go through it. Furthermore, such screening can help to prevent people who would find the procedures excessively demanding from attending a centre. In this instance, the use of tests for selection and development comes together.

Psychometric measures are given as an aid to self-development in many other settings as well, Typically, they are administered to managers on training courses so that the latter can see their results and have an opportunity to discuss the implications for their personal approach to work. Personality measures such as the Myers-Briggs Type Indicator[R], OPQ[R] and the Cattell 16PF[R] are all frequently used in this way.

Finally, tests have been used as an aid to the development of teams as well as individuals. For example, Belbin (2004) and others have argued that when members of a work-group have been selected on the basis of having complementary personality characteristics, they may perform more effectively than randomly constituted groups, even when the latter are intellectually more able. So, for example, the ideal management team would not only have the appropriate skills in specialist terms (eg finance, operations, HR, sales and marketing) but would also complement each other in the way that they would work together at a particular problem. It should be noted that although Belbin's ideas about team types are widely known and discussed, the research on which they are based is relatively limited.

HOW SHOULD THE TESTS BE ADMINISTERED?

Testing procedures have become increasingly streamlined over the years. Originally, many tests were administered orally to an individual one-to-one. More recently, group pencil-and-paper testing has become common because of ease of administration. The latest development is test administration and scoring on PCs, often via the Internet. Furthermore, with some tests, the items administered to an individual candidate can be tailored according to his or her speed of response and ability (correctness of responses). The number of items can thus be reduced and time saved. The capital outlay involved on computerised testing is considerable but it does have attractions for major organisations that handle large numbers of applicants each year (see Chapter 11).

SHOULD INTERNAL AND EXTERNAL APPLICANTS BE TREATED IN THE SAME WAY?

There are two main arguments for adopting different policies towards internal and external candidates, in terms of the tests to be taken and the scores considered to be acceptable. The first argument can arise when internal candidates already have experience bearing on the job for which they are applying, so that the amount of learning and adjustment they will need to make may appear to be small, and when it can be argued that assessments of performance on related jobs may be a good guide to performance in the new job. By contrast, the demand on external candidates new to the organisation may appear to be high. Accordingly, it might be proposed that testing should be carried out only on the external applicants. In deciding, much will depend on the ease or difficulty with which the transition has been made by past internal candidates and the confidence that can be placed in the assessments of performance.

Two issues must then be thought through with care. First, will test scores (and other aspects of the selection procedure) simply reflect job experience (or lack of it)? Second, could there be a danger that the procedure will 'pass' internal candidates who lack the potential to develop further?

A second argument for treating each group differently is that there is a stronger case for providing internal candidates with feedback on their performance in the selection procedure since it is important to sustain the motivation of employees who have been rejected. No doubt many external candidates would also like such feedback, particularly when they have taken a substantial test battery lasting several hours or even a day – they should be given it whenever possible (see Chapter 7).

TESTING OVERSEAS

Further issues can arise if organisations are recruiting overseas for staff to work in the UK, and if they are both recruiting and employing staff overseas.

If the recruitment is of staff to work in the UK, it can be argued that staff should be assessed on the same basis as UK applicants. This could mean that English-language versions of tests are used even if English is not the first language of applicants. Although this approach might not be 'fair' to all the applicants, legal and other problems are unlikely if the selection process is for work in the UK. However, by making practice examples and other information about the tests available in advance, steps can be taken to ensure that applicants are likely to obtain scores close to their true levels of ability.

Issues are more complex if the selection procedure is held overseas for employment in the same country. On the one hand, an employer may wish to use tests already employed in the UK for several reasons – for example, the tests are proven, and the scores of overseas applicants can be compared directly with those in the UK. On the other hand, issues of language and culture may mean that direct comparisons cannot be justified. One way of addressing such a situation would be to work with a test publisher that has significant experience overseas – for example, some tests and questionnaires are already available in a variety of other languages. Considerable expertise is involved in this adaptive work, and employers should not attempt it themselves.

Attitudes towards testing vary greatly throughout the world and it cannot be assumed that what is regarded as good practice in the UK will be welcomed or even accepted in other countries. For example, in South Africa there is particular emphasis on being able to show that tests are fair across races and cultures, and the legislation on it is enforced!

ANTICIPATING ALL THE CONSEQUENCES

At first sight the idea of having an organisation that is full of competent people is an attractive one. However, the introduction of 'better' selection may bring unexpected problems. An example follows.

CASE STUDY 11

An excess of success

At an engineering company it was tradition that apprentices who scored above a certain mark in their final examination should be offered work as trainee draughtsmen. Normally, one apprentice reached this high standard – sometimes none, sometimes two or even three.

Following the introduction of a series of aptitude tests to improve the quality of the apprentice intake as a whole, virtually the whole intake reached the required standard and the tradition had to be stopped.

Selection must be considered as a whole, as shown in the following example.

CASE STUDY 12

Selection taking 'too long'

In an organisation with well-developed selection methods, the processes were seen to be too slow by local operational managers keen to replace staff who had left. As a result of their pressure the local personnel manager dropped recruitment standards in order to take on more people – only to find that they couldn't do the work and he was under even more pressure for having taken them on.

7

Choosing tests and introducing them

Tests can be used to help assess a very wide range of people and types and levels of work, ranging from general management to functional and technical specialists, and from apprentices and other trainees to chief executives.

This chapter examines:

- critical issues to be considered before tests are chosen, taking account of the four As:
  - availability,
  - appropriateness,
  - acceptability, and
  - administration.
- issues of planning and implementation, including
  - (i) getting agreement to proceed with testing,
  - (ii) communicating testing policy
  - (iii) organising testing,
  - (iv) maintaining a large-scale testing programme,
  - (v) testing individuals, and
  - (vi) evaluation.

The starting point must be (a) the job description and (b) the person-specification for the vacancy or vacancies to be filled. However, there may be a number of qualities that might be tested and there are certainly a very large number of tests available.

It will become clear that a large number of issues must be taken into account. Decisions can be further complicated when tests are required to select for a job grade (involving a wide range of activities) rather than a specific job, and a way of addressing this issue is described in a case study.

We have focused on the use of tests for selection, but the same principles apply if questionnaires or other selection methods are being considered, or if tests or questionnaires are being considered for other purposes (eg career development, team-building).

BEFORE TESTS ARE CHOSEN

Before tests are chosen it is important to have a clear idea of the range of qualities or characteristics required for successful job performance. This in turn depends on a detailed appreciation of the work to be done. Information about the work to be done is normally collected together as a job description, while the qualities or characteristics required for successful job performance form a person-specification. Selection methods, including tests, then have to be chosen. Each stage is discussed in turn.

Job descriptions

The main purpose of a job description for selection purposes is to identify the tasks and activities that are crucial to the successful job performance. From this information, the qualities required in an ideal applicant (the person-specification) can be assessed by a deductive process. In addition, the job description should provide information about features of the work likely to attract (or even deter) candidates, including hours of work, pay, etc. Such information can be shared with candidates, ideally ahead of the final selection process, so that a degree of self-selection can occur.

It is rare to find comprehensive and up-to-date job descriptions waiting to be used for selection purposes, and more often than not information has to be specially collected. This is traditionally done using a checklist to cover salient features, such as the aims and objectives of the job, responsibilities, resources available, and so on. It is normal, too, to involve current job-holders, their bosses, etc, so as to build up a detailed picture.

In practice, the amount of detail to be collected depends on the number of vacancies to be filled and the importance and complexity of the job. If the vacancy is important, there are a number of special techniques that can be used to make sure that a comprehensive picture is obtained. Examples of the main types of techniques, which can be used singly or in combination, include:

- interviews – Staff may use a structured process such as Flanagan's critical incident technique, Kelly's repertory grid technique, or perhaps internally developed structured questionnaires that have particular relevance to the type of work being done

- job analysis questionnaires – These have been developed as a result of extensive research and continuous modifications. Examples are McCormick's position analysis questionnaire for lower-level jobs, and an equivalent version for supervisory and management jobs. Some of these questionnaires are now computer-administered, the results being analysed and printed by expert systems

- checklists – Checklists aimed at obtaining the fullest possible information about jobs have been developed – eg Toplis (1970)

- diary techniques – This involves the incumbent keeping a diary of his key activities over a long period.

However the information is collected, it is then important to consider which are the key activities and issues – perhaps the things that the recruit must achieve in the first year if the appointment is to be regarded as being a success. This is the essence of the 'critical incident' approach, but with some other techniques it is possible to end up with lots of detail but without any clear indications of priorities.

The person-specification

As described earlier, the person-specification comprises a list of qualities to be sought in an ideal applicant; it is based on inferences made from the job description about the personal qualities required.

Again a checklist approach can be of advantage in terms of helping to make sure that nothing important is missed. In the past a framework called the 'seven-point plan' was widely used in the UK. Devised by Professor Alec Rodger (1953), it suggested that the characteristics required in the ideal applicant should be listed under seven headings:

- Physical make-up

- Attainments

- General intelligence

- Special aptitudes

- Interests

- Disposition (personality)

- Circumstances (domestic, mobility, family connections, etc). Note that in the light of subsequent equal opportunities legislation, any questions in these areas should be confined to exploring job-related issues such as availability and mobility rather than circumstances *per se*.

From the information collected in the job description, the person-specification is deduced for each of the seven headings. For example, for some jobs there may be requirements in terms of height and weight – entry requirements to the police service are often cited as an example. However, it should be noted that any arbitrary requirements may be challenged on the grounds of unfair discrimination – in the USA, for example, the height requirement for police officers is now based on the argument that they should be tall enough to aim a gun over the roof of a car while using the car as protection. Minimum requirements should be realistic and should relate to the demands of the job and behaviour required for successful performance.

In drawing up lists of this kind it is good practice to distinguish between *essential* and *desirable* characteristics. It is important not to have too many 'essentials' or it may be impossible to find anyone who meets all the requirements. Should this happen, matters will have to be resolved by, for example, relaxing some of the essential criteria, reviewing the pay or other benefits or even changing the way that the work is to be done (see also Chapter 8).

When drawing up the person-specification it can sometimes be helpful to identify any contra-indicators – that is, features that may make some applicants unsuitable. For example, regular commitments in the local community might be a contra-indicator for a job involving frequent travel away from home, unless of course the applicant is prepared to change his or her lifestyle. However, in practice what matters is that the applicant is able to take on frequent travel away from home, and not any other details of the candidate's lifestyle.

When using checklists, such as the seven-point plan, it is normal to specify at least one characteristic under each heading. However, there will of course be differences in the types of quality sought according to the nature of the vacancy to be filled. For example, in the selection of a senior manager, some of the skills, abilities and personality characteristics in the following list might be considered important:

- oral communication skills
- written communication skills
- emotional adjustment
- analytical ability
- fertility of mind
- flexibility
- drive
- planning and organisational skill
- social skill
- delegation and control.

Choosing the selection method

The next stage of the selection process is to choose the appropriate selection methods to assess the qualities considered to be important. Possibilities include:

- application forms
- references and other written reports
- interviews (individual or panel)
- psychometric tests
- psychometric questionnaires
- group discussions, simulation exercises, etc, in which candidates work together or compete with each other.

In addition, self-selection among applicants is encouraged by many organisations (see Chapter 6) so there is the issue of what information can be provided for candidates and at what stage. In general it is seen as good practice for people to be able to see where they may be working and to meet their potential colleagues ahead of the final stages of the procedure and any job offer.

A useful aid to choosing the appropriate methods is to draw up a matrix, listing the requirements (eg the headings from the seven-point plan) in a column on the left-hand side and the potential selection methods at the top of a series of columns across the page. A tick can then be placed in the appropriate cell(s) of the matrix for each method that provides relevant information for each heading, ensuring that each heading is covered by at least one method. It is preferable that more than one method provides information about each requirement so that there is a cross-check. Any inconsistencies can be investigated through a final interview, by careful scrutiny of any written data, or by following up references.

> **CASE STUDY 13**
>
> **Cross-checking information**
>
> In an assessment centre for general managers, the applicants were asked to attempt a written exercise involving figures, graphs and similar information.
>
> One of the applicants was a qualified accountant who made no use of the data at all. Earlier in the procedure he had been asked to complete a short numerical reasoning test and had obtained a high score.
>
> In the final interview he was asked why he had not made use of the data and replied that he thought that this would give him an unfair advantage over the other applicants.
>
> In a procedure designed to give candidates the opportunity to demonstrate their competencies the assessors were bemused by applicant's approach on this and other matters. He was not offered the post.

Tests and questionnaires are particularly valuable for assessing intelligence and special aptitudes under the seven-point plan framework, and for providing structured, quasi-objective data about interests and disposition. Apart from assessment centres (which often involve tests and questionnaires) the other methods have shown very poor reliability and validity for assessing these characteristics. In contrast, tests and questionnaires also have some limitations as when, for example, collecting data on availability for work or physical make-up.

An advantage of the seven-point plan is that there can be a clear link between psychometrics and the rest of the assessment process. A further advantage is that the reasons for any shortcomings and whether and in what ways they might be remedied can also be relatively straightforward. For example, a candidate may lack ability in terms of a specific aptitude.

That said, many selection procedures now use a competency approach of the kind described in Chapter 11. These focus on the activities and behaviours required for successful performance such as 'information collection' and 'problem-solving'. If an individual fails to meet the required standard for a competency, tests and questionnaires can sometimes offer an underlying reason why things might be that way (eg a candidate who struggles with numerical problem-solving may be found to have problems with basic calculations).

However, the extent to which a link exists between a test score, a personality scale and a competency can be contentious. For example, if the competency of numerical problem-solving is required, and the candidate demonstrates the required standards, how much attention should then be paid to the candidate's results on a numerical reasoning test or on a personality scale which describes the candidate's level of interest in numerical work? It is our view that these issues should be explored and discussed with the candidate.

CHOOSING A TEST

As noted in Chapter 1, there are over 5,000 psychometric instruments available in the English language alone, as well as the other methods of assessment described in Chapter 11. Even restricting choice to those available to non-psychologists, potential test-users face a psycho-metric jungle – a jungle with more than its fair share of predators! The route might be charted by four As:

- availability
- appropriateness
- acceptability
- administration.

Availability

One obvious constraint on choice is the availability of tests – whether the organisation has staff who are qualified to use them or whether the tests are obtainable by non-psychologists at all (see Chapter 1).

However, all the tests described in Chapter 3 (and many others) are potentially available pro-vided that people have been sent on the appropriate courses.

The restriction of supply to staff with specific training does mean that an organisation consider-ing using tests must first audit its own resources of staff who are trained in this area. Some staff may have been trained while working for other employers. Should there be few or none, how-ever, a decision has to be made on whether to invest in sending people on the relevant courses or to have a special course run for the organisation (both of which may mean a certain amount of delay) or to bring in consultant occupational psychologists (see Chapter 4).

Appropriateness

Imagine that a person-specification has been drawn up listing, among other things, emotional stability and extraversion as desirable attributes for the person appointed. Because the tests must be appropriate to assess these characteristics, the next stage is to survey what is avail-able. It may turn out that there is a whole string of instruments purporting to measure these qualities of emotional stability and extraversion. How then can a decision be made as to which of them is best and most appropriate?

Factors to consider include the following:

- evidence of reliability
- evidence of validity
- evidence of the use of the test elsewhere
- normative data
- consistency with equal opportunities
- leading-edge design features.

Evidence of reliability

The reliability of a test is a measure of its consistency (see Chapter 2). Any worthwhile test should be supported by evidence of this. It will normally be summarised in terms of a single figure ranging from 0 to +1, where 0 indicates a complete lack of reliability and +1 shows perfect reliability. If the figures were based on test/retest reliability, +1 would mean that each person in the group had got exactly the same absolute or relative test scores on separate occasions (see Chapter 2). Perfect reliability is never achieved, but in ability tests reliability of +0.75 or above, based on a sample size of at least 100, should be expected.

Measures of personality are subject to rather greater variation, which is understandable as the expression of personality is perhaps more susceptible to transient influence than is the demonstration of ability when individuals are doing their best to perform well on tests. For personality measures, a reliability of +0.65 or above, based on a sample size of 100, is acceptable.

Evidence of validity

Validity measurements are evidence about whether the test is measuring what it purports to measure, and different kinds of validity were outlined in Chapter 2. The measurement can be illustrated by the extent to which a test has demonstrated that it relates to some external criterion – as, for example, tests given to bank clerks might relate to their subsequent job performance.

Again, as in the case of reliability, the evidence is likely to be summarised in the form of a validity coefficient that ranges from −1 to +1. A correlation of +1 means that on a graph plotting test score against job performance for a number of individuals there would be a linear relationship between test scores and performance, so that the person with the highest test score has the highest job performance.

Figure 1 | **A graph showing a correlation of +1 between test scores and job performance. Each cross represents the test score/job performance for one individual. For simplicity only five individuals are represented.**

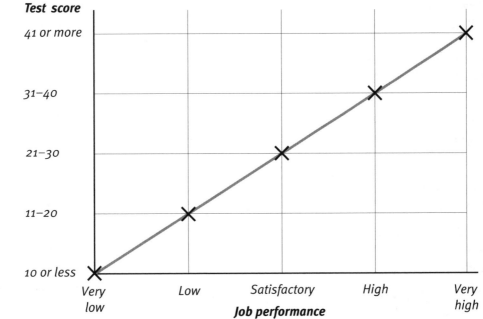

This is illustrated in Figure 1 on the previous page.

A correlation of −1 would reflect a pattern of scores in which the person with the lowest test score had the highest performance and the person with the highest test score had the lowest performance. A correlation of 0 would mean that there is no relationship between the scores and job performance.

Test manuals should contain data about validity. For example, the manual for a numerical reasoning test might show that for a sample of people selected for the job of bank clerk, the test scores correlated +0.35 with the ratings of performance made on those same people by their supervisors one year later. This would mean that there was a tendency for those scoring well on the test to perform well, but prediction would be far from certain.

The size of validity correlations quoted in manuals may at first sight seem low, but there are plenty of reasons – some of which are dealt with below – why it is unrealistic to expect high ones. For various technical reasons it is difficult to specify precisely what is and is not acceptable in terms of validity coefficients. Under some circumstances, validities as low as +0.10 might make worthwhile improvements to the effectiveness of selection, although correlations of +0.50 might be an initial target, and +0.20 a realistic goal.

Remember too that results from tests are often used in combination because successful job applicants have to be competent in several different ways. For example, an applicant for a clerical job might have to be competent at numerical calculations, understanding the meaning of words, filing, and carrying out simple instructions using tables of information. The four relevant tests might individually have rather low predictive power but together might reach an altogether more useful level.

When looking at validity information in test manuals, check the size of the samples involved in the validity study as well as the correlation itself (see below).

People who find it difficult to understand the implications of validity may find the hypothetical example in Table 1 helpful. Imagine that a test has been given to help select for a job. The test results are being validated by comparing the test scores with the number of promotions of each individual during the first four years. The table shows the percentage of people who achieved 0, 1 or 2 promotions during that period.

In the example, 40 per cent of the candidates who obtained a test score of 71 or above went on to achieve two promotions in the next four years, compared with just 10 per cent of those who had test scores in the 51–60 range. Increases in test scores seem to be clearly predictive of

Table 1 | *Comparison of test scores with the number of promotions over the initial four years*

Test score	Number of promotions gained in first four years (as a percentage)			
	0	1	2	
51–60	60	30	10	(100%)
61–70	40	35	25	(100%)
71+	25	35	40	(100%)

career success over the period examined. However, if you were given the test score for just one person, you can see that the data in Table 1 is by no means a perfect guide to the probable success of the individual with that score.

Validity evidence often has two components: the test score and the measure of performance (or criterion measurement). A wide range of criterion measures may be utilised, ranging from specific measures of task performance to rather broader indicators of success such as performance appraisal ratings, salary increases and promotions. None of these criteria is itself a perfect measure of performance. The promotion system in the organisation will not be 100 per cent accurate in identifying those most deserving of advancement, partly because in many cases the appraisal process to which it is linked is subject to all sorts of biases and imperfections. Using either promotions gained or appraisal ratings as the criteria by which the effectiveness of tests is judged is thus never going to yield a wholly accurate assessment of how good a test actually is.

Even when objective measures of performance are available, as is the case with many sales jobs, they seldom tell the whole story. The sales made have to be interpreted against the background of the potential of the territory, the competition, the manner in which the results were achieved (have claims or promises been made that will prove difficult to live up to and so make selling in that area more difficult next year?), and so on. But whatever their deficiencies, criteria of the kinds mentioned here are the best that are usually available and are certainly far, far better than no validation evidence at all.

In response to demands from potential test users for better information about test validity, test designers and publishers are starting to respond in two ways. The first approach is to offer computer print-outs detailing large numbers of correlations between tests and performance criteria. Some of these correlations will be high and will be offered as evidence of the worth of the test or tests. However, as indicated in the Preface, such information should not be accepted as proof. When a number of correlations are calculated, some large correlations will arise as random departures from zero underlying conditions – in other words, they will have occurred by chance.

Correlations are not explanations – remember that tomatoes are eaten by 98 per cent of juvenile delinquents! Remember too that a correlation between two groups of figures (such as a test score and a criterion of performance) can *always* be calculated – so the fact that a correlation has been calculated is not in itself proof of the worth of a test or questionnaire. What matters is that an appropriate method of calculating the correlation was used, the size of the figure obtained, and its statistical significance (see Chapter 10).

CASE STUDY 14

Statistical 'proof'

In the past a test publisher offered potential customers tables showing correlations between test scores and performance criteria. Accompanying literature implied that the figures showed the worth of the test. However, those with statistical knowledge could see that the tables actually showed that the correlations were too low and that the test should not be used for selection!

We suggest that test-users and others making decisions about tests should look for evidence of worth over and above the size of correlation. Four kinds of evidence might be considered:

- that specific hypotheses have been made and tested
- that an appropriate level of statistical significance has been used
- that there are theoretical or practical explanations for any large correlations that are found
- that similar findings have been found in independent studies.

The other way in which statistical data about test validity may be offered is in the form of a meta-analysis – that is, the results from validity studies published in academic journals are combined in order to assess the overall worth of the test. The names of Schmidt and Hunter are prominent in the literature: their approach has been based on the calculation of a figure for validity generalisation (transportability) dependent on two variables – the estimated mean true validity and the estimated standard deviation of true validities. These are relatively sophisticated statistical concepts and those who are interested in them may read further in the specialised literature.

In our view the technique is respectable in theory, but in practice caution should be exercised in applying the findings. One reason is that the findings from studies offered and accepted for publication in journals may not be typical of the results obtained for the test or questionnaire in general.

Occasionally, test-users may be faced with several alternative tests each with similar availability, reliability and validity. How then may a choice be made?

Under such circumstances, a decision may rest on the precise reason for requiring the tests. For example, if the primary purpose for testing is to assess suitability for a particular job, the ideal kind of validity evidence to be sought from the manuals of the test under consideration is that they have shown an acceptable level of correlation with some form of performance rating or other measures in identical work.

However, beware of deciding that work is 'identical' simply because a common job title is used (see Chapter 1), and be prepared to take professional advice, since differences may affect the worth of the tests significantly.

Where the aim of testing is wider, and the concern is to predict performance over a number of jobs that an individual might do in the first couple of years, and possibly to give some indication of career potential, the prospective test-user should seek evidence of correlations with performance measures over a period of time and with indices of progress (salary growth, number of promotions, etc).

The question, then, is whether the test has been shown to predict the outcome required. That said, however, the imperfections of each of the various performance criteria used are such that the more validation evidence there is, preferably including a range of criterion measures, the better.

Evidence of the use of the test elsewhere

Although it is important to know whether proper validation studies have been carried out, such studies are rare because of the sample sizes needed and the time and experience required. But while there may not be a wealth of validity data, the tests may be widely used and there may be considerable information about their use and acceptability which could influence a decision about whether or not to use the tests in particular circumstances. Enquiries to the test publishers, to consultant occupational psychologists and to experienced users, and reference to books and other publications describing test usage (eg Miller, 1975) can therefore be useful.

Some of the information may be positive. For example, major companies may comment favourably about the worth of the tests, about the ease of administration and scoring, and so on. Conversely, the information may be negative. For example, applicants elsewhere may be failing to understand instructions, test booklets may be found to have pages missing or to be poorly printed, and so on.

Finding that a test or series of tests have been adopted widely means that if they are given in the selection context, there is always the chance that candidates will have encountered them before. Indeed, because people tend to apply for more than one job at the same time, it is not at all uncommon to find candidates taking some of the same tests for different organisations in selection procedures just a few days apart. This inevitably carries the danger of familiarity breeding enhanced performance. For example, on the second and third presentations of an ability test candidates are likely to get marginally higher scores, but may not improve further thereafter. However, exceptions have been noted and test manuals should ideally give information on this point. In those instances where the individual has also been provided with feedback on the results of a previous assessment, this may considerably affect the attitude to encountering the same tests again. Personality measures may be particularly subject to distortion where a person feels the need to try to modify the picture that emerged last time.

Very widespread use of a test does carry with it this problem, and ideally, test publishers should provide information on the effects of previous testing both with and without feedback of results. Alternatively, users might aim to compile their own information. But at present if equally good but less frequently used measures are available it may be worth opting for them. Either way, it is good practice to check whether candidates have been through any similar procedures recently – and if they have, what tests were involved (they may not know the names, but the descriptions given will often give a good clue as to the identity). This sometimes enables users either to change the tests to be given or at least to be aware of some possible effect of prior experience. Unless the previous testing session was very recent – during the previous week or two – it is unlikely that scores on ability tests will be affected significantly.

Normative data

The use of a test elsewhere does, however, have advantages. It is of little value to know that someone has achieved a score of 56 on a test, where the possible range of scores is 10 to 75, without knowing how others compare with this individual's score on the test. In other words, normative data are required (see Chapter 2). An important factor in choosing tests is whether or not they can provide normative data relevant to particular needs. For example, an organisation selecting school-leavers for clerical jobs may want tests of numerical calculation and verbal ability that have normative data for 16-year-olds who have been entered for the highest GCSE grades. There would be little point in judging the school-leavers' scores by comparing them with the performance of graduates on the same tests.

Problems of some complexity can arise because abilities can influence career decisions and people tend to stop studying subjects in which they are making little progress. Imagine an engineering company assessing candidates for jobs in technical sales. Direct comparisons of candidates with an engineering or technical background with those of people who had a predominantly arts background might not aid a sound decision since as a group the latter would probably do significantly better on verbal and significantly worse on numerical or spatial ability measures than would the engineers. Over and above the test scores judgements would have to be made about the speed with which non-technical people might pick up technical knowledge, and the extent to which technical people might develop verbal sales skills. The availability of suitable training might be a key factor.

As far as possible, choose tests with norms that allow the comparison of like with like. The norms should also be based on samples that are large enough to give confidence that they are representative (at least 100, and preferably 200 or more). The manual that accompanies the test should contain that information. Although it is possible, and desirable, for an organisation eventually to build up its own norms, that clearly takes some time.

Consistency with equal opportunities

Another important standard by which to assess the suitability of any test is whether its use is consistent with equal opportunities legislation (see Chapter 4).

Leading-edge design features

Leading-edge or other design features may have particular appeal. One such feature may be adaptive testing in which each candidate is given a series of test items close to his or her personal levels of ability. Such testing, which is computer-based, can give a quicker and/or more accurate measure of ability. Another feature is the availability of the test in a form that can be administered over the Internet, thus enabling candidates in remote locations or working abroad to be screened at low cost (see Chapter 12).

Acceptability

Having run through some of the main aspects of judging the appropriateness of tests, it is time to consider the final element in the choice of process. This concerns the acceptability of the measures adopted to those being assessed. Factors to be considered include:

- the presentation of the test materials
- the face validity of the tests
- the acceptability of the test items.

The general presentation of the test materials

In earlier editions of this book we commented that poorly produced, dog-eared or drab test booklets do not endear themselves to candidates nor inspire confidence among clients or other managers. Accordingly, we felt that appearance should therefore be a factor in choice. Now our concerns are rather different – that slick design and speedy administration by computer or over the Internet may lead the unwary to assume that the test or questionnaire will be sound from a technical point of view.

That said, consideration should still be given to the apparent nature of the tests themselves.

- What are the people being tested likely to think the tests are for?
- How will they feel about what they are being asked to do or say?

The face validity of the test(s)

This refers to the extent to which a test looks as though it is measuring what it sets out to measure (see Chapter 2). Whether it looks the part or not is actually a very unreliable guide to the real, criterion-related validity of a test. But face validity does matter in other ways. With some ability tests there is little problem, since the type of intellectual ability being assessed is usually fairly obvious and knowing it will make scant difference to anyone's performance. Also, the rationale for giving ability tests is perhaps more readily (but by no means universally) accepted by candidates. Even so, some may want to use work sample tests with high face validity in spite of the cost of developing and using them and the problems of dealing with previous experience. (If a candidate lacks previous experience, will he or she be able to do the work sample test? If he or she has previous experience, will the test score simply reflect that experience rather than other important criteria such as the ability to learn or to progress?)

However, the rationale for using ability tests can be relatively straightforward compared with the rationale for personality measures. It is here that most of the trouble arises!

Developing personality questionnaires that have high face validity reduces the danger of alienating the individual who is being assessed. Such alienation might well have happened when, in the early days of personality testing in industry, applicants for normal managerial posts were asked to complete a personality inventory, much used in the USA, which included questions about bowel movements. Applicants might reasonably have wondered what on earth this was supposed to be assessing, and what relevance it had to the job in question. They might become increasingly annoyed at such an intrusive and seemingly irrelevant line of questioning, to the extent that a gut feeling of quite another kind would be telling them that this is not the kind of organisation in which they wish to work.

There are of course two problems here. One is the obscure purpose of the exercise and the other is the unacceptable nature of particular questionnaire items. Unfortunately, they interact with each other to produce a potentially unfavourable response. It is possible to construct personality inventories that are much more transparent and which thus are more likely to have higher face validity. People can see what is being measured and can relate it to the purpose of the assessment. In addition, such readily understandable measures are easier to use in any subsequent feedback session. Unfortunately, it also means that the candidates are in a better position to try to manipulate the impression they give of themselves on such measures – it potentially helps them to fake.

Turning to the problem of personality inventory items that may seem bizarre or extreme in some way, these are usually present as elements in scales that tap aspects of emotional adjustment – or maladjustment, to be more accurate. Or they may have the purpose of picking up people who are at the outer limits of some personality dimension (which again may have implications about the individual's adjustment in a more restricted sense). If personality measures are employed which avoid the use of such items, it will probably be at the cost of not assessing these aspects of the person as well as they might have done.

Incidentally, it should be pointed out here that some people do endorse extreme items of this kind; they do not always see them as being odd and do not cover-up (though equally obviously, some do!).

Opinion is divided about the best way forward, some taking the view that the candidate's self-knowledge is helpful, others distrusting it because they fear that some candidates will manipulate their replies. Accordingly, many procedures seek both to assess candidates and to give them the opportunity to report assessments of themselves. Some go further and ask the candidates also to assess each other.

If a choice is to be made, it should reflect particular circumstances. If it is of particular concern that those selected be emotionally resilient, because the jobs concerned are high-stress, then the balance may be felt to tip in favour of using measures that may be a little lower in acceptability to the candidate. In other circumstances, as when there is strong competition to recruit the best candidates, it might be felt that although there is still a need to assess them, it should not be done in such a fashion that it drives them into the arms of the competitors.

The acceptability of the test items

Consider how tests will appear to candidates. For example, when choosing personality measures the sensible thing to do is to go through the inventories and reflect on how they will seem to the candidates. Even if it is felt to be essential to use questionnaires that ask some of the more extreme types of question, there is still a great deal that can be done to minimise any adverse reactions. This is examined later in this book (in sections on the administration of tests and feedback of results).

Finally, under the heading of acceptability, the use of computers in testing must be considered. This is discussed in detail in Chapter 12.

Administration

Consider here the form or forms in which the test is available and the time that is required for administration. For example, if you are recruiting on a national or even international basis, you want to be able to administer the tests over the Internet. Another example is that in selection procedures are often tightly timetabled, and you may therefore want a test that can be administered and scored quickly whether by computer or in other ways.

CASE STUDY 15

Choosing tests to select for a job grade

In the real world it is rare to have sufficient information about an off-the-shelf test to be able to recommend its immediate and unqualified use. On the other hand, few employing organisations are likely to be prepared to spend months if not years waiting for the results of predictive evaluation exercises before deciding what test or tests to use.

One way of making a sound but relatively quick decision is to carry out a concurrent validation study. The following case study illustrates this approach in practice. Details are summarised from 'The value of test validation: a case study', a paper prepared for publication by Dr David Kellett, Ira Morris and Deirdre Fitzgerald while working for Psychological Services in the British Post Office.

The aim of the project was to recommend tests for the selection of clerical-grade staff involved in a wide range of activities, if possible from among the batteries available of off-the-shelf tests from commercial publishers because of the time and cost involved in designing a new test or tests from scratch.

The project began with job analyses of all the clerical duties in the main functional areas such as personnel, customer services, finance, operations, buildings and services. Psychologists carried out interviews lasting up to one and a half hours as well as working through the job components inventory, and a list of 29 activities was drawn up.

Commercially available tests were then reviewed in the light of the job requirements, and two test batteries – the Clerical Abilities Battery from the Psychological Corporation and the Modern Occupational Skills tests from Assessment for Selection and Employment (ASE) – appeared the most promising. These two batteries were then evaluated in detail against a number of quality standards (see Kellett and Toplis, 1989). Considering the contents of the test batteries, and evidence about their reliability, validity and fairness, it was concluded that the Modern Occupational Skills battery was the better suited on this occasion.

However, the Modern Occupational Skills battery comprises nine separate tests, all with high face validity. The next question to be considered was how many it was necessary to use. An analysis revealed that all nine tests were significantly correlated with each other, the highest being a correlation of 0.72. This was a clear sign that not all the tests would be necessary since, if two tests correlate highly, there is unlikely to be value in using both.

The next step was to compare scores on all the tests with supervisors' ratings of each individual's performance on the 29 clerical activities that had been identified. A technique called 'step-wise regression analysis' was used to see whether any other tests in the battery added significantly to the ability of the best test to predict supervisors' ratings of performance.

Results showed that a small number of tests appeared to be useful predictors of many of the supervisors' ratings – for example, two of the tests were each useful predictors of 11 supervisor ratings. In contrast, some tests in the battery were of relatively little value. It seemed likely that the best value for money would be obtained by using just three of the nine tests.

A final step before the tests were released for operational use was to look at the fairness of the tests. Insufficient numbers from the ethnic minorities volunteered to take part in the concurrent validation study, so the checking of race fairness had to be postponed until a predictive validation study could be carried out.

So far as the sex fairness of the tests was concerned, data were examined to see (a) whether there were sex differences in the mean scores, and (b) whether there were differences in the correlation between test score and performance according to the sex of those tested. Findings for the three tests that had shown most promise were:

	Comparison of mean scores (m/f)	Comparison of correlations (m/f)
Test 1	no difference	no difference
Test 2	no difference	no difference
Test 3	m slightly higher	m slightly higher

At the same time, data for all the other tests in the MOST battery were analysed in a similar way. Some differences were found with two other tests, which meant that they would have required careful monitoring had they been included in the final battery. These findings have been passed on to the test publishers.

In the light of the above findings it was decided to press ahead with the introduction of the tests. However, there were plans to monitor the use of the tests and to carry out a predictive validation study and investigate race and sex fairness as soon as sufficient data could be accumulated.

The study shows the value of careful preliminary work before tests are introduced. The nine tests in the MOST battery all have high face validity, and without the study it would have been impossible to say which tests were the more effective, how many were required in the final battery, and whether or not they required careful monitoring for race or sex fairness.

PLANNING AND IMPLEMENTATION

The final part of this chapter deals with six issues:

- getting agreement to proceed with testing
- communicating testing policy
- organising testing
- maintaining a large-scale testing programme
- testing individuals, and
- evaluation.

Getting agreement to proceed with testing

Assume that a stage has been reached where a strong case can be made for the use of tests as part of a procedure for the selection of graduate entrants (broadly similar principles would apply if other groups were to be involved). The recommendation to use tests could be based on a number of points, including:

- A follow-up of some recent graduate entrants in your organisation has shown that some have given up because of pressure of work while others have been given poor reports at the end of induction training and at the end of their first year of employment.

- An analysis of the work done by graduate entrants has been carried out and the qualities and skills required for successful job performance has been identified; from these analyses possible tests have been identified.

- The manuals for the tests show 'good' evidence of the worth of the tests for graduate selection – ie sample sizes have been over 100, and reliability and validity estimates have been satisfactory (see Chapter 10).

- The tests you want to use are similar to those used by other companies selecting graduates and to those used by your major competitors who do not seem to be facing the level of 'wastage' problems that your organisation is facing.

In most commercial and other organisations, the chances of gaining support for change are enhanced by proposals which estimate the financial benefit to be obtained. Ways of estimating the financial benefits that may be obtained from testing (and other selection methods) can be assessed by a technique called utility analysis. At its simplest the utility analysis formula is:

$$NET\ BENEFIT = QUALITY \times QUANTITY - COST$$

However, the background information required for the computation of utility and statistical formulae to be used are such that readers who are interested are referred to the specialist literature involving authors such as Boudreau. That said, readers may find it helpful to know that, other things being equal, the cost benefits from selection procedures are highest when one or more of the following apply:

- the validity of the selection procedure is high

- the selection ratio is low – ie there is a large number of applicants to choose from, relative to the number of vacancies

- enough applicants are of good/reasonable quality

- employees (in the relevant job) vary greatly in worth to the organisation – ie performance varies significantly.

There are some other issues that might also have to be addressed, particularly if a selection procedure already exists and possible improvements are being considered. Examples include:

- the acceptability of the procedure both to the applicants and those who are using the tests and other selection methods

- the extent to which candidates are learning from the experience of being assessed – in part this will depend on the feedback that assessors give them about their performance (see Chapter 4)

- the extent to which line managers are satisfied with the standard of those recruited – this can be particularly important if the managers cannot be directly involved in the recruitment of staff who will work for them, as might be the case in a nationally run graduate recruitment programme

- the extent to which business leaders are satisfied with the results – although their satisfaction may be based on opinions and impressions rather than scientific evidence about reliability and validity, perceptions are reality and should be managed accordingly.

If all these issues are taken into account in the proposals that are made, recommendations to introduce tests are likely to succeed. But even then it is possible that recommendations may not be supported or may even be resisted. For example, the number of applicants and the number of vacancies may not seem to others to justify the costs of staff being trained to use tests. Under these circumstances the case for using tests should be carefully costed and alternative strategies should be considered, such as the retention of a consultant or sharing the cost of selection with other companies through a group scheme.

Questions may be raised about the fairness of tests vis-à-vis applicants from ethnic minorities, those who do not match the prevailing sexual stereotype for the vacancy, and the disabled. Such questions may be anticipated if it is proposed to use tests for selection in organisations keen to advance opportunities for minority groups, and careful background research with the test developers and publishers may be required to establish the fairness of the proposed procedures.

The judgement that the use of tests will be beneficial may be challenged. Until the tests have actually been used in a particular organisation and results followed up, it is impossible to demonstrate the worth of tests with absolute certainty, and some may exploit this weakness in the case being put forward. Explanations involving probability and other statistics may impress some but infuriate others. For example, people who failed the 11+, whose sons and daughters failed the 11+, or those who feel that they were inappropriately placed during wartime or National Service may be strongly opposed to testing. In contrast, others may be supportive because of their past successes in selections involving tests, or because they have found career guidance involving tests useful for their children, etc.

Some may fear the consequences of better selection. For example, trainers may be concerned that courses may not be filled if higher selection standards are applied, while supervisors may fear the appointment of bright subordinates whom they will find difficult to manage.

So even if a case is technically sound there is no guarantee that proposals will be accepted. Some time should therefore be spent seeking the views of those who may influence the decision and making sure that the proposals embrace the points to which they are likely to be sympathetic and deal effectively with any objections. If written proposals are also to be presented orally, it may be worth holding back a little information about the potential worth of tests in order to strengthen the case being made on the day.

Sometimes it is impossible to make a strong case, as when no proven tests exist for the type of vacancy to be filled. Resistance can also be strong for this or other reasons. One way forward can then be to get agreement to a trial in which the tests are administered at the time of selection but the results are not used. Later, the test scores can be compared with performance as in a predictive validation study (see Chapter 10) and a decision about whether or not to use the tests for selection can be based on the results.

Communicating testing policy

If tests are introduced on a small scale to address a specific problem, the number of staff who need to know about this initiative might be relatively small. However, even at this early stage, key staff will have to be informed (and where appropriate trained), and candidates will have to be given test description handouts and information about how to obtain feedback.

If testing is to be used in a potentially sensitive area (eg for the assessment and development of current senior staff) or the numbers being tested at the time of selection grow, it will be appropriate to advise staff regarding the security/confidentiality of their test scores, how feedback can be obtained, the provision (if any) for retaking tests, etc. Some of this might be included in a staff handbook. There will be occasions, however, when it is necessary to brief staff about an initiative involving tests. The letter that follows was drafted for the chief executive of a charity who decided to use a development centre as a way of identifying a possible successor from among the charity's senior management team

---

DEVELOPING XXXXX AND ITS STAFF

One of the things that I do is to review how well XXXXX is doing and to think about how we can continue to develop so that we continue to be successful in the future.

Our efforts at recruitment earlier this year have made me realise what a good team we have managed to build up and develop, and as far as possible I would like all those currently working for XXXXX to have the opportunity to develop their potential with us.

For this reason I am inviting you, as a senior member of my staff, to take part in a one-day development centre towards the end of June. The centre will be based on the sort of centre that we ran for external candidates earlier in the year and will comprise

- tests and questionnaires

- a written exercise

- a group discussion

- a press interview

- a career review meeting with YYYYY, the consultant who worked with us earlier in the year. At

---

this meeting YYYYY will discuss your career to date with you and give you feedback about the tests and questionnaires that you have taken earlier in the day

- a final interview with me and with one of the trustees to discuss what has emerged from the centre, and our first impressions of what this might mean in terms of what you might do for us in the short and longer term.

After this, there will be a bit of a gap while everyone has time to reflect. I then expect to have at least one further meeting with you to discuss the possibilities that are emerging and how these might meet your needs. It is possible that we will ask YYYYY back to discuss those results which bear on how we might get the best out of each other when working together as a team.

One other thing – we plan to run the development centre immediately before a one-day procedure to recruit a new graduate. We believe that the results from the centre will give us a clearer picture of the sort of person who might best join us.

Please let me know if you would be willing to take part in this event by .... You have my assurance that the information gathered during the day will be treated in confidence. It is also important to let you know that my views about you are based for the main part on the day-to-day work that you do for me – however, if we are to plan for a successful future, we do need to take wider issues into account.

AAAAA
Chief Executive

Organising testing

Assume that proposals for testing graduate entrants have been approved. A training course in the use of tests has been successfully completed (or the services of an occupational psychologist retained) and it has been decided to use the tests as part of an initial sift – that is, only those short-listed applicants who reach a satisfactory standard on the test will be invited to the final interviews. What preparations are necessary?

First, thought must be given to the likely response, offer and appointment rates. Precise numbers and types of vacancy can be difficult to forecast and may change at short notice according to the latest business plans for expansion or contraction, changes in staff turnover rates, etc. In addition, when recruiting graduate entrants there is the problem of estimating how many of those accepting offers will actually start work and not withdraw their acceptance if a better offer arises.

Such problems are rarely appreciated by applicants, who are understandably annoyed if they reply promptly to advertisements only to find that all vacancies have been filled. They are particularly annoyed if they are successful during the initial part of a selection procedure and then find out that all the vacancies are filled before they have the opportunity to attend the final part.

Whatever the difficulties in making accurate forecasts, administrators must persevere with the best estimates available and try to avoid major errors. For example, there is little point in inviting all applicants for initial tests if it will be impossible to interview all those who are successful. On the other hand, if the number of initial applicants is too low and the numbers are then reduced because of the use of tests, the numbers being passed on to final interview may be insufficient. Past records may help to judge the numbers that should ideally be attracted, as may advice on the current state of affairs from careers officers, business contracts, advertising agencies, etc. It may be necessary to use suitable application forms (or design a supplement to an existing form) in order to sift on other relevant grounds.

Applicants should be told in advance what the selection procedure will involve – perhaps in the job advertisement, but certainly when sending out application forms and job descriptions in response to enquiries. Ideally, applicants should be sent handouts ahead of the procedure, which outline the kinds of tests to be used and give one or two example items for practice; they will then have time to seek further information from public libraries, from relatives and friends, etc. The handouts should also describe the selection procedure as a whole and answer any questions commonly raised by applicants. Applicants should be warned to bring spectacles and hearing aids if they need them.

Major employers such as the Post Office have printed leaflets for use in major recruitment programmes.

Testing should be carried out in groups of appropriate size: a test administrator should not normally test more than 20 people without assistance from other staff, although the precise number would depend on

- the level of appointment and type of test being used
- environmental factors, such as room size, and
- the testing materials available.

Level of appointment and type of test

A few applicants can feel threatened by some kinds of testing – an example might be an applicant for a top management post who has never seen a personality questionnaire but who has heard criticisms from others.

If testing is being carried out in circumstances in which good applicants are scarce, testing candidates individually or in pairs so that they can be greeted personally and given some individual attention is preferable to testing in larger groups in which individuals may feel anonymous.

Environmental factors

Minimum requirements include:

- fair space in a room that is large enough
- adequate lighting
- good acoustics
- a situation quiet and free from interruption
- comfortable seating

- a suitable work surface on which to rest papers, etc
- appropriate heating and ventilation.

The testing materials available

Some tests comprise question booklets and separate answer sheets, a format that enables the relatively expensive question booklets to be reused. The cost and availability of the booklets may influence the numbers to be tested at any one time.

Times for testing should relate to public transport times. Consider late afternoon or evening sessions for those still studying. Avoid clashes with examination dates. Check that there will not be any disruptions during testing, such as fire drills or major repairs in or near the building. Make sure that applicants will be properly received and that there are suitable refreshment and toilet facilities.

Ask applicants to confirm their attendance – allow time for this and specify a contact point within the organisation.

By way of an introduction to the testing session, briefing about the use of tests should be repeated and expanded as part of the essential process of settling the candidate down. People generally feel more at ease and in control of a situation when they know what is going to happen and when. This applies to testing as much as to anything else, and it is important to continue to work to overcome any anxiety that individuals may feel when faced with psychological tests. Indeed, the selection of those who are to be handling the test sessions should focus, among other things, on the ability of the people concerned to establish rapport with the candidates and to deal with them in a sensitive and socially skilled way (see Chapter 4).

Reputable tests have detailed instructions on administration, and these must be followed exactly. If the test instructions have to be read out to the candidates, the test administrator chosen must have a suitably clear and loud voice. If the testing session is a long one, time should be allowed for natural breaks.

If tests are being used as a sift, allow a sufficient period between testing and the final stage of selection for the tests to be marked and for those who are successful to be called forward: prior warning of the dates for the final stage of selection can allow the candidates to pencil in the dates in their diaries.

Records should be kept of all test scores (preferably the answer sheets as well) to facilitate follow-up studies to check the worth of the tests and of the procedure as a whole.

Maintaining a large-scale testing programme

Some organisations use tests on a large scale. For example, in the 1980s and 1990s, Post Office Psychological Services were supplying up to 80,000 tests annually to over 200 locations throughout the UK.

When providing tests for use in decentralised organisations, instructions have to be issued on all the above points, and staff trained. The following points also have to be considered:

- the supply of tests from a central point – in the case of printed test materials, stock control and distribution systems have to be implemented; with testing over the Internet there are issues about the security of the tests and the replies, how to check the identity of the person taking the tests, etc

- facilities for handling enquiries – for example, there may be enquiries from staff who are to administer tests and who have yet to attend formal training programmes

- systems for monitoring and inspecting the operation to ensure that good testing practices are being followed – steps must be taken to ensure that test materials are kept secure; samples of used test materials must be checked to make sure that they have been correctly scored, etc

- the confidentiality of the test scores and whether they can be used for other purposes (eg as part of an application for an internal post elsewhere in the organisation), and whether tests can be retaken by those who did not reach the required standard on the first occasion (see Chapter 6).

The following are illustrative of the kinds of problems that can arise in any large-scale testing operations:

- The recommended tests may not be given (eg shortage of time, not considered suitable by local staff, fear that much-needed new staff may be put off by testing).

- Other tests may be added or substituted (again both suitability and/or time required may be questioned by local staff).

- Inappropriate norms may be used for grading.

- Confusion may have arisen over pass marks (eg when instructions stating that 'grade 4 is a pass' are interpreted by some to imply that all those obtaining any other grade should be rejected).

- Local standards have been varied (lowered to fill vacancies or increased to keep numbers of applicants down) without regard to the requirements of the job and the future prospects for staff who are selected (see Chapters 5 and 8).

- Senior managers without training in the use of the tests may demand unsupervised access to test materials and to test scores; some may even wish to keep records of the scores for further reference, with plans to look at the test scores when reviewing the performance of subordinates or even plans to evaluate the worth of the tests.

- Staff whose work involves the use of tests may fail to master their administration and interpretation, and may be unable to convince local managers of the need to follow recommended procedures.

- Test materials may not be returned when the testing staff move to other work; left unattended they may become compromised.

Testing individuals

There are a number of possible reasons for giving tests to individuals – for example, the individuals may be applicants for top management posts, or even people from widely differing levels and backgrounds whose placement in the organisation may not be working out.

To promote as positive an attitude as possible on the part of those tested, it helps to foster a co-operative or collaborative perspective on the exercise, and it assists greatly if a confidential feedback session on the results can be offered, so that there is something in it for the individual (see Chapter 10). If appropriate, it can be worth pointing out that selecting people who are wrong for a job or who are not going to perform satisfactorily is probably not going to do them any favours in the long run.

Evaluation

Even if the initial choice of tests appeared to be a good, with plenty of technical and other evidence to support the decision, it is still important to evaluate selection methods after they have been introduced (see Chapter 10). Comparisons can then be made with results that might have been expected by 'chance' results obtained by 'leading-edge' organisations, by consultants, etc.

However, there are some aspects of evaluation for which 'before' and 'after' comparisons can be useful – for example, there may have been a wish to make a selection procedure more attractive to candidates as well as to improve it from a purely technical point of view. Accordingly, not only should the issue of evaluation should be addressed at this stage, but a 'wide' view should be taken going beyond purely technical features of the tests such as 'reliability' and 'validity'. All the objectives of the new (or revised) selection procedure should be noted, and if appropriate, current arrangements should be assessed or measured prior to considering further revisions.

8

Making and communicating decisions

Tests can be valuable in sifting large numbers of applicants to decide which are most likely to succeed in the final and more time-consuming parts of the selection procedure. Administration over the Internet and on personal computers can minimise the cost per candidate. However, considerable attention may have to be paid to establishing the cut-offs, and there is no single best way of doing this – indeed, there are a number of pitfalls to be avoided and the actual method chosen will depend on very particular circumstances. Results can also contribute to deeper assessments.

Personality questionnaires can also be used both for sifting and for deeper assessments. But again there are also potential pitfalls when using profiles from personality questionnaires. In particular, profiles from occupational groups are often based on all those who do a particular job, and not just those who are successful at it. The pros and cons of the statistical and holistic approaches to using personality questionnaire results are examined.

Ways of combining test results to increase their predictive power are outlined, and ways of integrating test results with other parts of the selection procedure are suggested. On balance, it is recommended that interviewers should know the test scores and personality profiles of applicants before they interview, so that the reasons for any apparent discrepancies can be probed.

Finally, the control of access to test scores is strongly recommended. It is also recommended that scores should not be stored for longer than five years unless follow-up studies are planned. Again, other possibilities are described. The importance of giving feedback to applicants – particularly those already working within the organisation – is noted, and ways of doing it are described.

Because of the vast number of tests available it is impossible to give detailed advice on the interpretation of scores on particular tests. What is possible is to give some basic principles that guide the use of test information in decision-making. They are:

- using aptitude and ability tests
- using personality questionnaires
- combining results to increase predictive power
- integrating results with other parts of a selection procedure

- access to results
- giving feedback on results.

USING APTITUDE AND ABILITY TESTS

With the advent of testing on the Internet and on personal computers, tests can be administered to large numbers of applicants at low cost. For this reason they are often given at an early stage in the selection process as an aid to sifting the applicants and deciding which of them should be called to interviews or other stages of the procedure that are more time-consuming (see Chapters 6 and 10). Used wisely, the strategy can have considerable commercial significance. For example, one large organisation used three senior staff to assess four candidates in depth during a day-long assessment procedure for key executive posts. When tests were used to sift applicants ahead of the day, an average of one in every four applicants was successful. However, on one occasion the initial sifting was not possible, the proportion appointed fell dramatically – senior staff made only one appointment from the twelve applicants seen in a three-day period.

In order to sift, cut-off points have to be established on the test or tests that are being used. This section describes how cut-offs can be set and examines some possible disadvantages of this strategy.

To illustrate the point, imagine that an employer is faced with a large number of young people applying for a two-year training scheme in engineering. In order to sift fairly and minimise the chances of failure during training, the work is studied and a decision made to use a test of mechanical aptitude. It is agreed that a personnel manager should attend a training course in the use of such a test.

Table 2 |

Mechanical aptitude test score	Percentile rank for applicant
30	95+
28–29	90
25–27	80
21–24	70
16–20	60
12–15	50
8–11	40
7	30
6	20
3–5	10
0–2	5

While attending the training course, the personnel manager is given the information in Table 2. Possible scores on the test range from 0 to 30, and based on a total sample (n) of 200 applicants to four other employers, the percentile ranks have been drawn up. (An individual's percentile score shows the percentage of applicants whose scores that individual has exceeded.)

There are at least five ways in which the personnel manager may decide on a cut-off for sifting in his or her own organisation:

- The first option is to press the test publishers for additional information about the use of the test elsewhere. This may yield recent information about the worth of the test being established for similar purposes.

- Second, it may be possible to get relevant information from local business contacts through CIPD meetings, etc. Staff of local colleges involved in training may know of other companies that use the same test. Of course, if the test is used widely among local employers, its effectiveness could be reduced through applicants taking it several times and becoming practised.

- Third, it may be possible to test existing trainees whose performance is known. It is naturally necessary to reassure those trainees that the test results will be used only as an aid to designing future selection procedures and will not affect their prospects. A potential problem here is that the existing trainees will not be as strongly motivated as they were at the time of selection, and this may affect their test scores. Further, the exercise will at best be a measure of concurrent rather than predictive validity (see Chapter 2).

- Fourth, a pragmatic decision could be made based on the numbers that can be accommodated in the final stages of selection and the likely final selection ratio. For example, it may be anticipated that one in six of those interviewed will be given job offers, and that three of every five offered jobs will accept. The numbers to be 'passed' can then be calculated once all the applicants have been tested.

- Fifth, the test could be given to applicants without the results being taken into account initially. Selection could take place on other grounds and then the progress of applicants followed up to see whether there is a relationship between test scores and performance, and whether a cut-off can be established. Although this approach has the advantage of providing information about what happens to applicants with low test scores, attitudes to this strategy will vary: some may welcome an objective trial but others may not be happy with the idea of taking on low scorers and waiting to see if they fail!

The actual method chosen will depend on circumstances. Factors to be taken into account include:

- the numbers of applicants and vacancies – With 1,000 applicants and 100 vacancies, the worth of the test can be checked on the intake for a single year; with 10 applicants and one vacancy, decisions will have to be based on the experience of test designers and others

- how effective present selection methods are – If they are good, it may be possible to let things run while the worth of the test is established. But if urgent action is required, arbitrary decisions may be necessary in the hope of improving the situation quickly

- how many applicants are coming forward – Can the numbers be increased? If there are many vacancies and few applicants, the use of tests as a sift may make recruitment even more difficult

- whether a minimum standard can be established below which applicants are unlikely to succeed

- whether a maximum score can be established above which applicants may be too able and present problems because they are bored.

Mention has been made of the possibility of following up the performance of those already recruited. In order to build up numbers this might involve data about the recruitment of employees over several years, but care must be taken in doing this. For example, if the standards of performance expected of employees has changed radically over recent years, it would not be appropriate to merge all the data and then look for trends. Rather, comparisons of the test results and standards of performance should be made for each year.

Returning to the earlier example of the engineering training, imagine that the data in Table 3 were collected about the trainees who had taken the mechanical aptitude test, at the end of the two-year training. Given the data below, the cut-off might ideally be set at the score of 25, so that the likelihood that those selected would finish their training is 95 per cent. However, this strategy would mean creaming off the very best of the applicants in terms of test scores, and it is important to check whether there are sufficient applicants to make this a practical proposition.

In this example, the need to check is confirmed by looking back to Table 2. Taking only those who scored 25 and above would mean selecting the top 20 per cent of applicants, so to find 20

Table 3 |

Mechanical aptitude test score	Percentage of entrants completing training
25 and over	95
21–24	93
16–20	86
12–15	82
8–11	75
6–7	68
6	20
5 and below	45

people who attained this level of performance on the test a pool of 100 candidates would be needed. Sometimes the term 'selection ratio' is used to summarise the situation. If only those scoring above 25 were taken on, there would be a selection ratio of 0.20 (the ratio of the number to be taken on, 20, to the number of applicants, 100).

But what if there are fewer than 100 applicants? One possible way to fill the vacancies would be to reduce the cut-off score. Thus, if there are only 50 applicants and 20 trainees are again required, the selection ratio would be 20:50 – or 0.40 as it would normally be expressed. To recruit 20 trainees from 50 applicants would mean that the crucial test score would be lowered to 16, as it can be seen that 59 per cent of applicants get a score of 15 or below, and 40 per cent get 16 or above. Going back to the data on the relationship between test scores and completion of training, the proportion of applicants getting a score of 16 or more that would be expected to finish the training would be 86 per cent. In practice, the cut-off score would have to be lowered still further to allow for the rejection of candidates who are unsuitable in other parts of the selection procedure. Although tests can be the most useful part of a selection procedure, they should never be used alone.

Sometimes the need to fill vacancies may lower the pass mark to a level at which the likely percentage of failures is unacceptable. One way of dealing with such circumstances is to put additional effort into raising the numbers of applicants by, for example, more advertising. Other alternatives might be to improve induction and other training, to redesign the work to make it less demanding, etc. Sometimes employers have arranged pre-training schemes aimed at those whose education and employment experience does not provide them with a good basis for either the selection procedure or the training itself. Pre-training schemes can also provide an entry route for those who have dropped out of school altogether.

By contrast, some employers are currently faced with the problem of having large numbers of well-qualified people applying for relatively undemanding jobs. In the absence of data showing a clear statistical relationship between scores and the criterion, such employers sometimes assume that 'you can't have too much of a good thing' and cut-off points are raised higher and higher. However, the assumption does not always hold. For example, several studies have shown that managerial performance correlates with intellectual test scores only up to a point – beyond that point, very high test scores do not seem to be associated with superior managerial effectiveness.

Quite apart from this kind of finding, the blind pursuit of high test scores may simply result in the selection of a group of people who are over-qualified for the job in question, and who will quickly become frustrated, bored or dissatisfied, and are then likely to leave.

USING PERSONALITY QUESTIONNAIRES

Although the examples given so far have been based on aptitude tests, the same issues apply when considering the results of personality questionnaires. Indeed, the picture here is even more complex. There are two broad ways in which such measures can be used. The first is in a holistic fashion, trying to get an overall picture of the individual by looking at the pattern of scores and examining the interrelationships between the different traits.

So, for example, a manager given a personality questionnaire may have produced a profile that indicates high levels of emotionality and aggression. This does not necessarily mean, however, that the individual concerned will frequently display these dispositions in an overt way. We might find that other scores suggest that he is actually a very restrained person who exercises firm self-control, and that he has a high level of objectivity and insight, indicating that he is unlikely to be all that easily offended. Only by taking account of the wider pattern of personality scores can the implications thus be seen for how the person will behave.

This approach to interpreting personality data is sometimes called the clinical or holistic method, because it reflects the way a psychologist might use the information in trying to gain a deeper understanding of the personality of one particular individual. To be effective, it calls for considerable skill and experience, along with an underlying knowledge of the psychology of personality. The alternative to this – which is generally used in organisations – is to take a more statistical, even mechanistic, approach. Here, the objective is to avoid having to do much actual interpretation of the personality scores, and instead to be guided by the empirical relationships already established between the scores and various criteria of job success. The aim is to select people who have the kind of personality questionnaire scores that are associated with effective performance – irrespective of any possible interrelationships there might be between individual dimension scores. There are several versions of this way of using personality data, involving cut-off scores, 'danger zones', and profile-matching.

Taking the first of these, cut-offs, there are similar dangers to those mentioned in relation to ability scores. Suppose, for instance, that a personality questionnaire has an emotionality scale, and that an organisation has found (or believes) that high scores on the scale – indicative of high anxiety levels – are associated with poor performance. It might be tempted to introduce a cut-off score to screen out applicants who are anxiety-prone or unstable. But what about people who score at the other extreme on this dimension, very low scorers who seem to lack emotions and feelings? They may be highly insensitive and tactless, unable to empathise with those around them. Presumably the organisation would not want to recruit many of them (particularly in some jobs), yet by using a simple cut-off it would fail to weed them out.

An increasingly common way of dealing with this problem is to establish so-called 'danger zones', which in effect are upper and lower cut-offs. A company might, on the basis of the correlations it has found between some personality measure scores and job performance, determine that people who fall below a specific level on any one dimension are unlikely to be successful. Yet it might also recognise – perhaps on a commonsense basis as much as anything – that extreme scores in either direction are probably contra-indicative of success. So it establishes a range of scores within which candidates are acceptable, but above or below which they are rejected. This is an increasingly common method, and one that is both flexible and relatively easy to use. It is not without its problems and dilemmas, however. For example, how does one compare a candidate who has fallen inside a danger zone on, say, two of the eight scores and who looks very good on the other six, with a candidate whose scores are only just within the acceptable range on all eight dimensions? There is no easy answer to this – it is a judgement call.

The third type of statistically based approach to using personality questionnaires involves the development of profiles for specific jobs or occupational groups. Scores on personality inventories are often put together to produce a profile chart that shows the individual's position on each dimension in relation to the average score and in terms of the distribution of scores as a whole. This is a very popular way of summarising the basic facts. The background against which the person's score is portrayed may be the norms built up for that organisation or they may be the norms as supplied by the test producer in the test manual. Sometimes, as in Cattell's 16PF, the well-known personality questionnaire, there is quite a range of profiles available showing the score patterns for different occupational groups.

The profiles appear so convenient and helpful that it is easy to overlook some important considerations in using them. The first is that to be of any real worth, the norms presented in the profile must be based on adequate sample sizes. Groups of 40 or so are just not large enough to be confident in the stability of the data; groups of at least 100 are essential, and groups of 200 or more are to be preferred.

The second danger is that the norms used may not be appropriate. For example, it might be most appropriate to compare graduate applicants for general management with each other and/or applicants 12 months earlier. To compare them either with those actually taken on 12 months earlier or with graduates applying for sales posts could severely mislead.

The third danger is of thinking that the profile represents a picture of what is desirable and effective in terms of personal qualities for that group rather than simply what is typical. Profiles from groups of scientific researchers can illustrate that this is unwise. On the 16PF, these groups can be characterised by, among other things, tender-mindedness (or emotional sensitivity). But in studies that have focused on an index of effectiveness – in this instance the number of publications the scientist produces – it has been found that the more effective members of this group are actually characterised by tough-mindedness.

What occupational group profiles present is a picture of what is typical of people who have stayed in a particular job and perhaps adjusted to it. However, their experiences of the job might well have affected their replies and hence their profiles. So one problem is that group profiles reflect concurrent validity rather than the preferable predictive validity (see Chapter 1). Further, group profiles often do not differentiate between those in the group who are performing well and those who are not. It is of course possible to develop separate profiles for the successful and unsuccessful sub-groups, and this more detailed information is required for effective selection decisions.

In this section, the main approaches to using personality questionnaire results have been outlined (a refinement of the statistical approach, using regression analysis, is mentioned in the next section). What was described as the clinical approach relies heavily on the expertise of the person doing the interpretation. Its advantages are that it uses all the information yielded by the questionnaire, and that it can provide a richer and deeper understanding of personality than can the more mechanistic techniques described above. However, because it relies on interpretation, this approach is also inevitably more subjective in nature, and where there is more subjectivity, there is greater scope for error (Highhouse, 2003). This is the main advantage of the statistically based use of personality questionnaires – it minimises subjectivity and reduces the need for skilled interpretation, thus rendering it more widely usable.

Because there is no one 'right' way of using personality inventory information, and all the alternatives have their strengths and weaknesses, what is the personnel practitioner to do? Much will depend on the purpose the questionnaire is being put to, and on the available level of training and expertise in the use of the instrument concerned. In general, the 'danger zones' approach will probably be more appropriate in large-scale selection exercises, and the clinical, interpretative approach will be needed when dealing with individual cases. An extremely valuable compromise between the two is where personality scores are used to highlight areas of doubt about candidates (perhaps because of some scores falling outside the acceptable range) and to raise other questions or hypotheses concerning their personality make-up which can then be followed up by, and probed in, an interview. We return to this matter shortly when examining the integration of test results with other parts of the selection procedure.

Before moving on, it is important to describe the distinction between *ipsative* versus *normative* personality measures. This is a somewhat technical issue, but briefly it revolves around two different approaches to personality measurement. Whereas normative test scales are independent (so that, for example, your score on the anxiety scale is not affected in any way by how you answered questions on the sociability scale), ipsative test scales are not. The latter, in effect, invite the respondent to make choices between the relative strengths of different personality qualities in their make-up. In other words, they do not compare the individual with other people: they produce a picture of how dominant different tendencies are within a single person. The 16PF is an example of a normative test, whereas the Concept versions of the OPQ are ipsative (some versions of Concept are normative). Both approaches have their merits, but the problem comes when they are used interchangeably, particularly where an ipsative test score is used to compare people as if it were a normative one. A full description of the two approaches is beyond the scope of this book, and the reader is referred to Johnson, Saville and Fletcher (1989) for a succinct look at the question. However, it is certainly important to find out which type a personality questionnaire is, in deciding whether it is appropriate to your needs.

COMBINING RESULTS TO INCREASE PREDICTIVE POWER

The complexity of most jobs makes it unlikely that a single quality will determine success and therefore that a single test will be adequate to assess applicants' suitability. The question then arises of how to combine tests together into a battery. One way is to use multiple cut-offs, so that the tests are taken in a series, only those individuals who have exceeded the critical score on the first test going on to take the second, and so on. In practice this is a rather cumbersome process and likely to be used only in a limited range of circumstances (generally where there is a multiple-stage screening procedure).

The other way of using tests together is sometimes called the composite score method. This involves the use of complex statistical techniques – multiple correlation and regression analysis – that are beyond the scope of the present examination. In effect, this method takes the individual correlations established between each test and the criterion, and between the tests themselves. It finds what is the best combination of test information for predicting performance and other criteria, and yields a set of weights that can be used in future, which gives the correct emphasis to each piece of test data to maximise the accuracy of the prediction. The composite score approach to combining tests often shows that the power of a battery of tests is much greater than the individual test validities might indicate. Several separate tests may have correlations with the criterion in the 0.1–0.2 range, but a composite score may produce a correlation of 0.4 or more.

This approach can also be used to identify which particular traits within a personality questionnaire are the most important in terms of prediction. For example, it may be found that administrative ability, drive, work commitment, emotional stability and sociability, as measured by a personality inventory, all correlate more or less equally with some indices of sales success. However, it may well be that there is some degree of intercorrelation between these scales. The use of regression analysis can identify which of them is most important in predicting success, and how they should be individually weighted and combined to yield the best prediction. It could quite easily be that work commitment and sociability are the main predictors, with emotional stability adding a lesser (but still useful) amount of predictive power, and the other two trait scores being redundant. How is it that these last two – administrative ability and drive – could be of no use when the original analysis showed that they seemed to correlate well enough with the criterion of sales success? Simply because they both correlated strongly with the work commitment scale scores, and their relationship with sales success was entirely due to this, rather than to anything extra they added for themselves.

The above assumes that an organisation has some data on the relationship between test scores and whatever it is that it is trying to predict. Often, that is not the case, so there is no opportunity to find out what the optimum weighting for each test should be. This should not deter the organisation from using a battery of tests and combining the results together on a more intuitive basis to build up a picture of the candidate. Evidence shows that although this is not as effective a way of using the information to predict future performance as is statistical analysis, it can still produce impressive results (Bentz, 1985; Moses, 1985). The range of abilities and qualities that must generally be considered is in itself a convincing reason for the use of a battery of tests, provided that the battery does not become so large that it is more a test of endurance than of anything else.

INTEGRATING RESULTS WITH OTHER PARTS OF A SELECTION PROCEDURE

When the main stage of the assessment is reached, a number of questions arise. First, if testing and interviewing are to take place on the same occasion, is it worth arranging the testing so that the results are known before the interview starts? In our view, tests are best administered before any interview, so that the results can act as a source of hypotheses that interviewers can probe and test in the interview. This is the approach taken in the assessment of candidates for the most senior posts in the UK's Civil Service, for example. Any marked traits or deficiencies might be singled out in this way, especially in relation to personality characteristics. Also, any discrepancy between the level of intellectual potential (as shown by the tests) and the individual's level of achievement should be the source of close scrutiny.

There is a counter-argument that maintains that the test results should not be available before the interview so that the interviewers are not biased in their judgements by the information. There is some force in this, but overall the balance is definitely in favour of using the results to guide the interview – there are apt to be a lot of queries hanging in the air afterwards if they are not. Further, it is difficult to resolve these issues once the candidate has left.

Another issue is how much weight to give to the test scores compared to other sources of assessment data, such as academic record, references, interviewers' ratings, and so on. In practice, some users place too much weight on test scores and others too little. With regard to the interview, much depends on how it is carried out. A structured, competency-based interview is likely to achieve reasonable validity and less adverse impact (Weisner and Cronshaw, 1988; Huffcutt and Roth, 1998), whereas the old-style personnel interview has repeatedly been shown to lack both reliability and validity.

The value of references is even more questionable. Although some studies of references have shown good validity (eg university references about graduates sent to the Civil Service Commission), many have not (Reilly and Chao, 1982). Moreover, recent changes in the law have made many individuals and organisations reluctant to give them at all. Their main value probably remains in helping to establish that the person is actually who he or she says he or she is!

Academic records and other background facts about the person can contribute significantly to accurate prediction when treated statistically and put together in the form of a 'biodata' questionnaire – although this is just mechanistic prediction and does not say anything about the individual as such. By themselves, facts about academic achievements have proved very variable predictors and generalisations are particularly difficult to make. In part this is due to the fact that differences in grades can reflect small differences in marks, that there are different pass rates in different subjects, that there are different examination boards and syllabuses, and also – in recent years – the tendency of so many students to get the highest grades, so reducing the discriminatory power. Psychometric tests commonly predict future performance better than do academic results.

The wisest strategy is to gather assessment information from a number of sources rather than to rely completely on any one. This can be done by using person-specifications and/or competencies as frameworks and drawing together information from tests, questionnaires, performance appraisals, etc. No single source (including psychological tests) will be perfect or anywhere near it, but in combination they can provide strong evidence – for example, high reasoning tests scores combined with a strong written exercise and high academic achievements can be a persuasive combination. Where discrepancies in the findings from these sources arise, they must be investigated thoroughly. In general it should be remembered that the test data is likely to prove the more objective and predictive.

From all that has been said so far on the subject of using tests in decision-making, it should be apparent that there are considerable dangers in trying to interpret results in an entirely mechanistic fashion. But this is precisely what some assessment reports generated on computers do – the test or questionnaire data are fed in and the machine produces a series of statements that appear to be justified by the individual scores rather than by groups of factors or the total profile. This is examined in more detail in Chapter 12.

ACCESS TO RESULTS

The increasing use of psychological tests brings with it the danger of the abuse of the information they provide. Controlling access to that information is one way of reducing the danger, and once testing has taken place the records must be placed in the agreed systems. Ideally, test results should be available only to the individual assessed (in the course of a properly conducted feedback session, of which more anon), to an HR manager trained in their use, and beyond that on a limited 'need-to-know' basis. Assuming that the HR department is arranging the assessment, any access to the results given to line managers – who are likely to be untrained in testing – should be carefully monitored and guided by the HR manager concerned. Failure to do this is likely to lead to a fair range of horrors, from excessive reliance on the findings (and probably wrongly interpreted for good measure) to complete disregard of them. There should certainly be no question of copies of test results or the reports written on the basis of them being held anywhere other than by HR, and access should be restricted to accredited users. Completed answer sheets and profiles are confidential documents and must be treated as such.

How long should the results of tests be kept and referred to? Some major test-producing companies say only 12–18 months, but this may reflect a desire to 'play safe' or to sell more tests rather than a frank assessment of the speed at which people change on what are, after all, supposedly stable characteristics. A rule of thumb would be to say the test data have a 'shelf life' of five years and no more than that.

People do change over time, of course, and to dig out test results from 15 years ago when making a decision about an individual – which has been known to happen – is neither fair nor sensible. Personality data is more prone to variation than are ability scores, although over a very long period there may well be a tendency for verbal ability to improve while other ability scores decrease somewhat. There will be big individual differences in the extent of change over time, some people showing marked changes and some virtually none. That said, circumstances change more rapidly than people, and it is this that might dictate when retesting is appropriate – because if the demands and setting role have shifted markedly, either different tests may now be appropriate or the original ones should be taken again and interpreted against the new background.

However, data more than five years old should be kept as a source of information about the worth of long-term procedures, such as identification of potential top managers among graduate entrants. One final aspect to this question – quite apart from the people changing – is whether the characteristics of the test itself (eg the psychometric properties of its items) change over time. Remarkably, they have been found to remain consistent even over a period as long as 16 years (Chan, Drasgow and Sawin, 1998).

If tests are being used as the sole basis of sifting, a five-year gap would seem to be far too long and a much shorter interval would seem appropriate. For example, the policy in one large organisation was that existing employees seeking promotion could attempt the tests and questionnaires twice within a two-year period. There were two reasons for this policy. First, some employees had a fear of such tests and it was felt that the opportunity to take them again could help reduce the pressure that they experienced. Second, some employees were making the effort to change their scores and profiles in the light of feedback – for example, by studying fractions, percentages, etc, or by reflecting on interpersonal style – and it was felt that they should have the opportunity to show whether development had taken place.

GIVING FEEDBACK ON RESULTS

Throughout this book there has been a great deal of emphasis on the reactions of the person taking the test and on the need to make the experience as acceptable and as stress-free as possible. This is particularly important when internal applicants are being assessed, since good feedback (perhaps with an individual's results being discussed in relation to the kind of competency framework described in Chapter 11) can help to sustain the motivation of those who have been unsuccessful. However, there is growing recognition that feedback to external candidates is also important because it should help to make the process more attractive to them and increase their perception of procedural justice (Ployhart and Ryan, 1998). Further, one of the surest ways of securing honesty in answering questionnaires is for the candidate to know that there will be some feedback.

Ideally, feedback should be given by someone trained both in testing and counselling – it requires counselling skill to present results that are not always very positive in such a manner that the individual concerned is both accurately informed of them and still able to maintain motivation and self-esteem. See Fletcher (1985, 1997) for further discussion of this.

If at all possible, the feedback should be treated as a confidential discussion so that it does not become an extension of the assessment process in the eyes of the candidate. A fairly common approach to sessions of this kind is to start by seeking the candidate's views and feelings about the tests, then to go through them one by one – always checking that the tests being talked about at each stage are recalled by the individual and that he or she is given the opportunity to comment on the results.

When the basic test data have been conveyed, the discussion moves on to interpreting them in terms of their implications for the individual's behaviour and relationships at work, development needs, career progression and aspirations, and so on. The more the candidate can be encouraged to participate in this interpretation and discussion, the better it is likely to be. It will be in the organisation's interests as well that employees or potential employees who have undergone psychometric assessment should be able to use the information obtained in seeking to improve future performance.

It is sometimes possible to give feedback on some aspects of performance (eg test and questionnaire results) during an assessment or immediately afterwards, and this can increase motivation to attend. But there is a strong case for delaying most of the feedback until the outcome of the assessment is known, particularly for internal applicants. The feedback will be much more meaningful if related to the new job or to the prospects for those who have not been successful.

In Chapter 9 there is information about the large-scale testing programmes carried out by major employers such as the Post Office and Civil Service. The question arises as to whether, and in what ways, feedback can be given to external candidates, particularly when very large numbers of applicants are involved and a very large amount of time might be required.

In part the strategy of the testing organisation regarding feedback will depend on the type of test used. If, for example, applicants have attempted a test designed to measure computer programming aptitude which has been used as a first sift, a letter telling applicants that they had not reached a sufficiently high standard to move on to the next stage of the procedure might at first seem adequate. However, it would be helpful to candidates to know whether their rejection was because there were too many candidates with higher scores or whether they simply did not meet the minimum standards. From the point of view of the candidate this could make the difference between trying for programming work elsewhere and making applications for a different kind of work. Some candidates like to ask questions of someone trained in testing and counselling skills in order to obtain any additional information. (For example, was the failure 'borderline'? Is the aptitude test widely used?)

Although contact by letter or telephone might suffice if a particular skill is being tested, complications may arise if either a range of qualities are being tested or if the candidate has taken part in a more complex procedure such as an assessment centre. Here, the potential problems in giving feedback would seem to be even greater because of the very detailed information that has been collected. But the demand for feedback from the candidates is also likely to be high because of the time and, in some cases, personal information they have given. The problem is that there is more likelihood of the applicant being 'hurt' by the knowledge that he or she has failed to reach the required standard in this wider assessment process. Indeed, there is evidence (Fletcher, 1991) that there can be long-term adverse consequences for psychological well-being in such circumstances. It is one thing for a person to learn that he or she has not got the aptitude for a particular job, quite another for the person to receive information which suggests that he or she has little potential for a whole range of jobs! However, simply to avoid giving feedback does not help the candidate who could benefit by learning about areas of relative strength and being reminded that there are many jobs for which the particular tests and exercises used would not be relevant. Again, the telephone number of a good trained contact person might be given. The alternative, where feedback on the results is given face to face to the candidates via trained counsellors and/or a designated member of the assessor team, is obviously expensive but is sometimes employed (especially with internal applicants).

A form of feedback that can do more harm than good is simply to send a written copy of the test results or of a report on them to the individual without any amplification. Apart from the fact that things can look a little stark in print, the person concerned is almost certainly untrained in testing and knows next to nothing about what the scores really mean or how the interpretations are arrived at. The scope for misunderstanding is formidable, and there is a good chance that the recipient will be upset by some of what is said. With no opportunity to seek elucidation or to explore the implications of the results with someone who is properly trained, the individual may be worse off than if no feedback had been given at all.

9

Using tests with top managers and other senior staff

Tests can undoubtedly make a contribution to the selection and development of top managers, and in individual instances can be the source of considerable insight into the capacities and potential of candidates. However, in general the success of top managers depends on a large number of issues and on their ability to display evidence of combinations of knowledge, skill and behaviour. Accordingly, the importance of individual test results should not be overstated. Although, at their best, such test results can help to identify issues and to crystallise themes arising from other information, there is little to be said in favour of using test results in isolation, and much to be said against it. As in most selection situations, a combination of methods is likely to produce the best result.

Much of the early work with tests involved their use on a large scale, either to select staff for government, for the military or for groups of vacancies such as apprentices or clerical workers. However, in more recent times there has been increasing use of testing in connection with the selection of top managers and their development. For example, the multinational company ITT put in place an executive assessment programme for its most senior people way back in 1959, and this acted as a model for many other applications of psychometric testing at this level for some while after. By the early years of the twenty-first century, however, this practice has extended to many other senior groups, including top civil servants and professional staff.

In this chapter we examine the selection of top managers and outline some case studies. There are also sections on individual and team development and on the role of testing in other approaches to development.

THE SELECTION OF TOP MANAGERS

In our view, work on the selection of top managers should be approached in the same way as any other kind of selection assignment – that is, it is essential to obtain a clear understanding of the work to be done, the issues to be faced, and the factors that are critical to success. It is also important to learn about the wider context of the post – the make-up of the team, the skills and development needs of those who will report to the post-holder, the culture of the organisation, and whether and how it should be developed or changed, etc.

Given a good understanding of the vacancy and of the qualities required in a successful candidate, appropriate selection procedures must be identified. At this level it is important to assess whether applicants can demonstrate their ability to do the job as a whole, since top management is about using combinations of knowledge and skill rather than using individual skills on their own. (If you are in any doubt about this assertion, would you fly with a 'pilot' who knew about aircraft and airports, about engines and fuel, about navigation and communication, and about instruments and controls, but who had never actually flown before?)

Tests of the kind described elsewhere in this book can be used in a number of ways, including:

- to help shortlist the applicants
- as part of the main selection procedure
- to assess the most promising candidates.

Testing to help shortlist the applicants

Some management posts attract hundreds of applicants. However, careful preliminary work on the nature of the vacancy and the sort of person required to fill it may mean that short-listing is relatively easy. For example, it may be decided that certain kinds of experience and achievements are essential and only candidates with these experience should be short-listed.

At other times the vacancy may be one that could be filled by people from a wide variety of backgrounds – an example might be the post of chief executive of a small business or charity in which the work content is of a fairly general nature and a highly specialised background is not essential.

Whatever the applicant's background, it is often a key requirement that the successful applicant is able to 'hit the ground running'. Indeed, senior appointments are often made at a time of crisis when there are financial and other problems. The ideal applicant thus offers knowledge and experience as well as potential.

A systematic approach to short-listing usually involves an interview to clarify and amplify the candidate's application and to check his or her track record and achievements. In addition, tests and questionnaires may be administered at this stage, and this might usefully done by consultants or agency staff recruiting on behalf of others. In contrast, if those responsible for making the appointment are involved in short-listing, there are other possibilities too which reflect the key requirements of the vacant post. In the case of the chief executive of the small business or charity these might include:

- making a short presentation about how to take the business/charity forward, and answering questions
- completing a business or other case study – perhaps using a personal computer rather than handwriting.

There are other possibilities but a compromise must be struck between the information ideally required and the length of meeting appropriate at this preliminary stage. Often it is felt that two or three hours of the applicant's time is the practical limit.

Where one is dealing with much larger numbers of applicants – for example, the Prison Service when selecting for prison officer jobs – tests are sometimes used as a preliminary assessment step between the application form and being short-listed for interviews or assessment centres. Most often these are tests of cognitive ability, but sometimes personality measures and biodata are used to sift. Indeed, with the advent of Internet testing (see Chapter 12) this is becoming more common. Although there are arguments in favour of such practices, the evidence is that using tests in this rather remote way (there is little contact with the organisation) to determine who shall go forward for consideration tends to be the least popular form of testing with the candidates themselves (Fletcher, 1997).

Testing as part of the main selection procedure

Various assessment elements may be used at the final selection stage for senior posts where candidates are seen and considered individually. Again the emphasis tends to be on finding candidates who can 'hit the ground running', and methods may include:

- a business case study requiring a 'written' report (again a personal computer might be offered); questions are then asked about the report
- a presentation about how to take the business/organisation (much broader) forward; again questions may be asked
- role plays, including mock press interviews
- completing relevant tests and questionnaires
- one or more interviews to discuss career history, professional/technical skills, managerial skills, etc.

The reason for seeing candidates individually is to maintain confidentiality – many senior managers do not want to let it be known they are considering moving. In those relatively rare cases where an organisation is completely open about top appointments, it gives them the opportunity to bring candidates together as a group to directly compare their performance. Possible advantages of doing so are:

- to see whether candidates can display interpersonal and other skills in practice
- to be able to relate behaviour and performance with other aspects of the selection procedure such as test results; this can indicate whether applicants have a good understanding of their abilities and development needs, the way that they come across to others, etc.

There can be times when group activities of this kind yield little information because the participants are so polished in their interpersonal skills as to give little away – but trained assessors can often pick up hints and clues to be followed up elsewhere in the procedure. There is the further complication that it is normal to treat applications in the strictest confidence and this cannot be guaranteed if the candidates are to meet each other. Accordingly, if it is wished that the candidates should meet, they should be told of the proposed arrangements in advance.

Testing to assess the most promising candidates

Individual assessments by occupational psychologists or other consultants are sometimes sought as a final check before a key appointment is made. Typically, the kind of assessment processes at this level involves a battery of tests covering cognitive abilities and personality, as well as an in-depth interview. It would normally be carried out by a very experienced assessor, and last 4–6 hours. (Often this is the maximum amount of time available, and even that may be hard to arrange for people with demanding senior roles.) Obviously, the level of difficulty of the cognitive tests used and the norm groups for the measures have to be chosen to be appropriate for top-level management. The resulting assessment report may be structured in terms of the specific competencies relevant to the job, or focus on particular queries raised about a candidate, or take a more general view of the individual. An example of such a senior-level assessment report is given in Appendix IV.

Two issues sometimes arise in testing top-level candidates, and both in a sense relate to track record. The first is that some senior people resent the use of cognitive ability tests – their thinking is along the lines of 'I have surely proved I have the mental horsepower needed already, without all this!' This is even more likely to be the reaction if one is dealing with a member of a highly qualified professional group (eg selecting for a senior corporate lawyer position). They have a point, too, especially as beyond a certain threshold level of intellectual ability the evidence suggests that personal qualities are more important in determining further success. It is important to show some sensitivity to this, and each case must be reviewed on its merits. If the field of candidates is very varied in terms of formal educational achievements and kinds of organisational experience, it may be wise to include cognitive measures. If, however, they are all double-firsts from Oxbridge who have worked their way up the career ladder to senior positions in government departments, it may not – quite apart from anything else, one might find they all scored within an elevated but restricted range, offering little on which to discriminate between them. However, even in the latter case, or something like it, there are still arguments in support of using cognitive measures. For example, has the individual long since reached his or her intellectual ceiling and is he or she now running to stand still? Has he or she any intellectual reserves to be able to advance up a level? There are also special cases (see Case study 17, below).

The other track record issue arises specifically with internal candidates. They often think, and sometimes say, 'Doesn't the company know enough about me by now to make up its mind without tests?' Again, there is some justification for the question, but the usual reason that organisations seek assessment of internal candidates is that they want an independent, unbiased view of the individual, and they also want all the candidates (whether internal or external) to be assessed against the same standards.

Whereas senior-level staff are perhaps more ready to challenge and ask questions generally about an assessment process, this is especially true of scientific and professional staff. The assessor must be ready to face questions on the validity of the process and of the tests used. Candidates with a strong science background in particular are likely to ask about the evidence for the value of tests. This is not necessarily a defensive reaction – it is just part of their normal intellectual approach and often simply reflects interest and curiosity.

Finally, one of the main reasons for having assessments done by consultants external to the organisation, apart from any possible lack of such expertise internally, is political. It is not usually considered acceptable for a potential member of top management to go through such a sensitive and probing procedure conducted by someone who may soon be one of their sub-ordinates. Also, experienced external consultants will be able to benchmark the assessment against industry standards at this level of seniority, and they should also have the credibility to handle the feedback to the candidate in a manner that is acceptable to them.

Case studies

Some short case studies illustrate issues that can arise in the selection of top managers:

CASE STUDY 16

Responding to a 'new selection method'

A consultancy organisation approached the chief executive of a major employer claiming that they had a new method of selecting top managers. Each candidate was asked to look at drawings through a tachistoscope [an apparatus resembling a camera shutter] and to describe what was seen. It was argued that 'good' managers would describe all the features of the drawing, whereas 'poor' managers would ignore aspects of the drawing that they did not expect to be there. The test had been based on the principle of perceptual defence – that because of the mass of information that we receive, our attention has to be selective, and this selectivity can mislead or distort.

In addition to this method, candidates were also interviewed at length.

The chief executive was impressed by the novelty of the approach and asked his chief psychologist to comment on the procedure.

In turn the chief psychologist sought advice from a psychologist who had expert knowledge of the subject of perceptual defence. She expressed surprise that the tachistoscope was always working at the same speed and that no attempt was made to calibrate each individual's speed of vision before starting the test. She could find no evidence of insight arising from the technique in the sample.

The chief psychologist reported this to the chief executive, emphasising that there was no independent evidence of the worth of the technique in the selection of top managers. The chief executive was clearly intrigued by the idea – but when he learned about the high fee requested for assessments using the unproven technique he quickly lost interest.

Although this cannot be regarded as a comprehensive review of the technique, it raises the question whether all methods used to select top managers are valid. The same sorts of question can be raised about the use of graphology in management assessment, the evaluation of graphology being further complicated by the fact that most practitioners in the UK belong to one of three different schools of graphology with contrasting approaches and interpretations.

CASE STUDY 17

Investigating poor test results

A telecommunications company asked an external consultant to assess an applicant for a director-level post. The test results were surprisingly negative, particularly on the ability tests. 'These results can't be right,' was the company verdict – 'He's got a wonderful track record!'

They asked that he be retested, which he was, but with the same poor performance.

The company was perplexed, and was considering disregarding the test result, when it emerged that the individual concerned had an alcohol problem, and one of some long standing. The first reference checks had not picked this up. It was beginning to affect his intellectual functioning, which was reflected in the test results.

CASE STUDY 18

The need to maintain confidentiality

A financial services organisation commissioned an occupational psychologist to assess a candidate for the post of IT director. The assessment report was duly sent to the personnel director, as a confidential document. He then circulated the report around several other managers within the organisation, without further explanation. They had no experience of such assessment reports and no frame of reference to guide their interpretation of what they were reading.

In these circumstances, considerable misunderstandings can arise, and a particularly unfortunate consequence of this was that one of the line managers read out the report over the phone to the executive search consultant who had proposed the candidate.

The result was that a very garbled and inaccurate account went back to the candidate before he had attended his formal feedback session, which not surprisingly left him feeling rather upset – partly because of the misinterpretation and partly because of the lack of control over access to this sensitive material about him.

This is an example of how important it is to try to maintain appropriate levels of confidentiality in relation to top-level assessments, and also to make sure that those who do see them have the necessary guidance or experience to be able to understand them.

For other practical aspects of handling the 'politics' of the external assessment process, see Fletcher (1998).

TESTING, COACHING AND INDIVIDUAL DEVELOPMENT

Tests can be used to help individual top managers develop. A crucial aspect of this is, of course, giving them feedback on their test profile, and talking through the implications of this both for the kind of roles they are suited to now and for the direction they take in the future. In doing so, it is important to identify what strengths they have in order that they can build on them and choose roles that play to them – although often (and perhaps less effectively) there is even more focus on where their weaknesses lie and what steps they can take to improve on them. Although the latter is worthwhile, it is important to assess which development needs are most likely to respond to training and experience, and what kinds of development would best suit the individual. Indeed, in some cases this is the underlying question of the assessment – how much potential does the manager have to develop further?

It is not uncommon for senior managers who are unsure of where they should focus their future career to be referred (or even themselves to ask) for an individual assessment, and this may take place as an early element in a longer-term coaching programme. In this context it is possible to use tests in an increasingly refined way. Having obtained a general picture of the individual's profile, more specific tests can be used to focus on particular areas where additional information is needed to assist in the development process. For example, a broad personality questionnaire might highlight various traits and the sort of leadership style that the individual might be inclined to adopt. There can then be discussion about the advantages and limitations of the style, whether the individual can appreciate and use other styles, etc.

TESTING AND TEAM DEVELOPMENT

Tests can provide insight into team behaviour and performance. For example, questionnaires which help to assess the likely style of individual team members can help to identify areas in which individuals might clash, areas in which the team as a whole may have limitations, and so on. Some of the measures used for this are individually focused (eg the MBTI and the Firo-B), but there are also others that are designed specifically to assess aspects of team functioning, like the Team Climate Inventory (Anderson and West, 1994). However, it must be remembered that such questionnaires depend on the self-perceptions of the team members. If these are not accurate, there is the further question of how individuals can be helped to see themselves more accurately. Skilled facilitation may be required if the test results are to help individuals to consider the possibility of modifying their style for the benefit of the team as a whole, and the team is to move forward.

THE ROLE OF TESTING IN OTHER APPROACHES TO DEVELOPMENT

Some approaches to development involve a combination of individual and group work. For example, one of us designed 'development workshops' for the top managers in the British Post Office. The workshops had seven features, the combination of which is believed to be unique. The seven features were:

1   An overall model was developed to help people to take stock of themselves and to produce an Individual Development Plan for the future. All the elements of the workshop were clearly related to the model.

2   There was work for the participants and their line managers to do before attending the first of two workshop sessions so that they could get the best out of the time that they spent at the first workshop. An example was the Learning Styles Questionnaire designed by Honey and Mumford – participants were offered a personal report on their learning styles from Alan Mumford himself.

3   Each participant's line manager attended on the first day of the first workshop. This gave the opportunity for the line manager and participant to compare views about (a) competencies required in the participant's current job, (b) the participant's strongest and weakest competencies, and (c) competencies likely to be required in top Post Office managers in the future.

4   'Career architect' materials were utilised. Based on American research into generic management competencies, the following materials were used: (a) 67 cards, each describing a management competency and giving indications of how the competency might be 'over-used', (b) 19 cards describing 'Career stoppers' (behaviours that have been shown to hold people back in their careers if not addressed), and (c) books linking each competency with development activities.

5   Action Learning sets (groups) were utilised. Participants worked in Action Learning sets on at least three occasions, sharing plans and ideas and offering each other support and constructive criticism. The sets were facilitated by leading external consultants to give additional insight and experience and to ensure confidentiality.

6   There was an interval of some six weeks between the two parts of the development workshop. This was to allow time for the participants to clarify information about their competencies, their values, possible development opportunities, etc. A panel of experts was available to offer help and support on an individual basis, if required. It was at this stage that tests were sometimes used to help individual managers to clarify their development needs, or to clarify possible plans for the future, or a combination of both.

7   Participants met for a further 30 hours to share the work that they had done when taking stock and to start to prepare their plans for the future. By the end of the workshop they were expected to have drafted an Individual Development Plan. Following the workshop they were asked to finalise the Plan with their line manager and to send it to the Director of Management Development for the Post Office.

The use of tests as part of development activities or programmes is also examined in Chapter 11.

10

Evaluating tests in a time of change

This chapter describes three possible ways of establishing the worth of tests, and then shows how checks can be made to confirm that the tests are discriminating fairly. The benefits, costs and potential problems involved in testing have been drawn together under the following headings:

- the potential financial and other benefits
- the main potential costs
- other risks and possible costs.

In this chapter we address in more detail issues initially raised elsewhere in this book:

- How can the technical worth of a test be assessed – ie is it valid, and at what level?
- Does the test discriminate fairly?
- Assessing the benefits and 'downsides' of testing (financial and other benefits compared with costs and potential problems).

Once again, the main focus of comments is on the process of selection.

ASSESSING THE WORTH OF A TEST

Validity is perhaps the most important factor to take into account when evaluating a test, for if the test does not measure what it claims to measure, the procedure is pointless. However, to say that a test is 'valid' means no more than that predictions can be made from the results in a way that is better than chance. It does not tell us how good the test is, how test results compare with other selection methods, etc, and for this reason statistical measures of validity are highly desirable; the most commonly used statistical measure is the correlation, which ranges from −1 to +1 (see Figure 1, page 69).

In an ideal world, the level of validity of the test or tests chosen would have been already established during a number of similar applications, and the potential confirmed by trials in which the tests were administered at the time of selection, but no account taken of results. Following such preliminaries it would be possible to assess validity with some confidence. However, the ideal is rarely achieved.

For example, consider how an aptitude test for computer programmers might be chosen. First, the work being done by the particular group of programmers would have to be considered – programmers work on different kinds of problems using different computer languages (software) and different computer equipment (hardware). If a test is a predictor of the performance of just one group of programmers (working on one type of problem using a single language and with one manufacturer's equipment designed three years ago), with what confidence can validity be assumed for other groups of programmers?

Other issues can also affect the level of test validity, including the age, educational standard and test sophistication of the applicants. So in an ideal world, studies of the validity of the tests would be carried out on an ongoing basis by the organisations using them, even if evidence of validity elsewhere is strong.

There are various approaches to validation that can be taken. The first relates to predictive validity, which is regarded as the best single measure of the worth of a test (see Chapter 2). However, there are very few people who have the technical expertise to carry out a proper study of predictive validity, and there are a number of methodological and statistical pitfalls that can give misleading results to those who lack professional qualifications and expertise. Nonetheless, there are three reasons why those who use tests should have *some* understanding of some of the steps involved in assessing validity:

- The first is that an understanding of the basic principles will help with the initial choice of tests and/or with the choice of expert advisers.

- The second is that it can be helpful for HR managers and others to appreciate the kind of information that will have to be recorded and collated if validation studies are to be carried out.

- Third, it is important that HR and other managers know how the worth of tests can be monitored so that they can seek expert advice if there are signs that all is not well.

So it is desirable for an organisation to do some studies of limited scope for itself. There are two main kinds:

- subjective evaluation studies
- studies involving summarising data.

Advice on statistical analysis is also given below.

Subjective evaluation

An initial form of validation that needs no statistical analysis, but which nevertheless has some worth, is to consider how the test results match up to observations. If an employee is tested, do the findings 'make sense' in terms of the experience of the person concerned? While the tests may point up some features or ideas about the individual that are new (if they did not, it would seem to have been fruitless asking for the tests to be done, unless for reassurance), the picture that emerges should not be unrecognisable. When evaluating test results by looking at the way a person behaves once he or she has been taken on, a danger to guard against is the self-fulfilling prophecy – in other words, people may see only what they expect to see. If the numbers to be followed up are very small, this may be the only kind of analysis that is feasible, but more rigorous approaches should be used if possible. Certainly, conclusions should not be reached without taking informed advice.

Studies which involve summarising data

Data that can be collected is essentially one of three kinds:

- biographical data
- data about test scores
- data about job performance.

Biographical data have to be collected because one of the most important principles of summarising data is to compare 'like with like'. Test scores may depend on characteristics of those doing the tests (such as their age, sex, ethnic origin), whereas their job performance may depend on their length of service, education and many factors other than test scores. If numbers are small (fewer than 100), there is a danger that the sample may not be representative, and any trends must therefore be viewed with caution. Sometimes numbers can be increased by pooling data – for example, by combining the test scores of applicants at different sites or over several years, but it is best to take expert advice if pooling is necessary. If numbers are sufficient, the data should be examined to see whether there appears to be a marked difference between, for example, the test scores of women aged under 20 and those of men over 45. If there are marked differences, the groups should be kept separate when doing further analysis (see below).

Data about test scores must be collected to look at both the number of scores and their range. In order to check the worth of the test it is desirable that the actual test scores cover the full

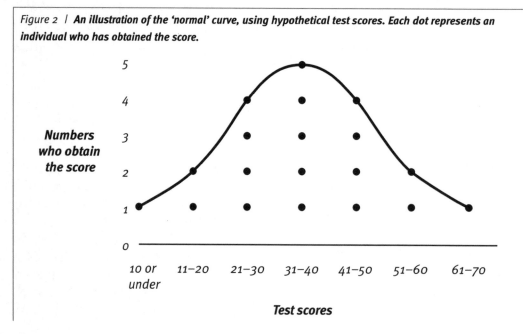

Figure 2 | **An illustration of the 'normal' curve, using hypothetical test scores. Each dot represents an individual who has obtained the score.**

range of possible test scores, and that when drawn on a graph, the pattern of scores approximates to a bell-shaped curve called the normal curve (Figure 2). If selection decisions have taken the test scores into account, there may be few, if any, people with low test scores among those taken on, and for this reason the curve may not be bell-shaped. To determine whether or not there is a full range and distribution of test scores, look at the shape of the curve, compare the scores of those recruited and those rejected, and compare the patterns of these scores with those for other groups reported in the test manual.

Next, data about job performance have to be collected. The following are possibilities:

- ratings from managers or supervisors
- time to first promotion
- number of promotions gained
- salary growth
- tenure (length of stay)
- absences
- successful completion of training
- sales achieved by the individual.

Ideally, several of these measures should be used: otherwise, there is a danger of the tests being selected on the basis of their ability to solve one problem (eg reducing the number of low performers being taken on) but at the expense of another (eg a rise in labour turnover).

As with test scores, it is important to look at the distribution of the data that have been collected. For example, it may be found that all those recruited are judged to be at least satisfactory and that few, if any, are judged less than satisfactory or unsatisfactory.

The final stage is to plot on to a series of graphs information combining test scores and job performance. If possible, each graph should comprise similar groups of people (eg females under 21) which are often referred to as sub-groups. These sub-groups can then be combined to form larger groups (eg all females).

Having drawn a series of graphs (or, if the numbers are small, just a single graph), the pattern of scores should be appraised. If the scores approximate to a line (straight, curved or even bow-shaped), use can be made of this pattern to predict job performance, and the test is almost certainly valid and reaching an acceptable level of validity.

If there is no pattern to the test scores, look back at the range of distributions of both the test scores and the measures of job performance. If the scores or measures do not cover a full range, the results may be inconclusive because, for example, it cannot be predicted how people with low scores would have performed if they had been recruited. Expert advice could then be sought on the application of statistical corrections.

If there is no pattern to the scores and there is a full range of test scores and measures of job performance, there may be problems – and it would be wise to seek advice from an occupational psychologist and/or the test supplier or publisher. However, remember that in large-scale recruitment programmes testing need be only a little bit better than chance to be commercially worthwhile, and that marginal trends can be difficult to grasp visually. Also remember that the rest of the selection process, such as the interviews, may not have been subject to the same scrutiny: do not assume that they would have been better predictors if they were!

Statistical analyses

The summaries of data described in the previous section can go some way to establishing whether a test is working. However, it can only take you so far, as these examples show:

Managers in one organisation compared test scores for apprentices with subsequent performance and as a result wrote an article claiming that tests supplied for apprentice selection were 'useless'. In fact, only those scoring in the top 5 per cent of marks had been recruited, but the lack of range of test scores had not been taken into account when validity had been assessed.

A manager in another organisation suggested changing the design of a test on the basis of two samples of test scores each less than 30 in number – and both samples came from the same office. The organisation was using 5,000 copies of the test annually, spread over a number of locations!

Many different kinds of statistical analysis can be carried out on data from tests and assessments of performance. One common analysis is to determine whether or not the results are statistically significant. A statistically significant result is one that is unlikely to have occurred by chance, and there is a convention of using asterisks (*) to indicate the level of confidence that can be placed in the results. The convention can be summarised thus:

*   means that the probability of a result occurring by chance is less than 5 per cent (using statistical convention, $p < 0.05$)

** means that the probability of a chance result is less than 1 per cent ($p < 0.01$)

***means that the probability of a chance result is less than 0.1 per cent ($p < 0.001$).

When looking at the results of statistical analyses many factors must be taken into account, including the appropriateness of the statistics used. In particular, note that:

- Small sample sizes make it less likely that statistically significant results will be found.

- Correlations may be of little practical value, even if they are statistically significant. For example, correlations less than 0.10 would not normally be regarded as worthwhile for selection predictions unless it was a very large-scale recruitment exercise.

- Correlations do not imply causation or explanations. For example, there might be a correlation between cups of tea drunk each day and take-home pay, but people cannot increase their take-home pay by drinking more tea.

Accordingly, it is recommended that expert advice is taken from occupational psychologists who specialise in test validation. An obvious source of expertise would be the organisation supplying the tests – in general, such organisations complain that very little data is made available to them for analysis. That said, if analyses are raising questions about the worth of the tests, it may be worth seeking a second opinion for an independent specialist. The British Psychological Society publishes a *Directory of Chartered Psychologists and Expert Witnesses*.

Coping with reality – a rapidly changing organisational scene

All the above advice is sound and the practices advocated desirable, but sometimes it has been prefaced with the words 'In an ideal world . . .'. We don't often inhabit that place! The pace of change in organisations – and even in society as a whole – is such that it may not be possible to evaluate tests as thoroughly as one would wish. What, then, is realistic and feasible?

It should certainly still be possible to carry out the subjective evaluation described. Also, it should remain worthwhile to collect the summarising data – which may be needed anyway to answer enquiries about fairness in selection (see below). But if a selection process is not going to be in place for more than a year or two before the job picture changes, some of the longer-term statistical validation may either be impossible (through lack of criterion measures of performance) or simply not worth doing. It may still be possible to look at the relationship between test scores and training performance, where the appointments do involve a formal training period (such as in a graduate training scheme), or at some other relatively short-term measure of performance that is available soon after those appointed have started work. This would give a quick indication, but it may not say much about the longer-term effectiveness of the individuals or of the tests used.

It seems likely that organisations will have to increasingly rely on two other sources of validity. The first of these is *validity generalisation* – which effectively means checking to see that there is evidence from elsewhere (preferably from a wide range of organisations and a wide range of jobs) that the test or type of test used has repeatedly correlated at an acceptable level with job performance. The point here is that if that can be demonstrated, there is a strong *prima facie* case for arguing that it is likely to be valid in this organisation too – the validity 'generalises' across companies and roles. (For further comments about validity generalisation, see Chapter 3.) The second source of support comes from *content validity*, which rests on the clear relevance of the content of the test to aspects of what the individual actually has to do in the job. For example, a numerical reasoning test based on interpretation of tables of financial data might well have content validity for some roles in banking and finance.

DOES THE TEST DISCRIMINATE FAIRLY?

Effective tests discriminate on the basis of job-relevant characteristics. Unfair discrimination – that which is based on non-job-relevant characteristics – should be avoided for a number of practical reasons, quite apart from its undesirability in ethical terms. For example, it can be challenged on commercial grounds. If an organisation is excluding large numbers of potential applicants because of their sex, ethnic origin, etc, it may have difficulty in filling vacancies and surviving in the future. In addition, it is important that any organisation aiming to provide a service for a wide cross-section of the community should be sensitive to a range of needs. Unfair discrimination can also be challenged because it is illegal and because suspicion of unfair discrimination can lead to costly enquiries. For example, employment tribunals can be costly both in terms of meeting damages or other awards and in terms of the time the staff may need to pre-pare for the tribunal and to attend it. Further, there can be adverse public relations implications affecting both the perceived worth of top management and the attractiveness of the organis-ation to potential employees (see Chapter 4).

Checks should be made to ensure that tests are not discriminating unfairly against:

- members of one sex
- members of ethnic minority groups
- disabled people
- applicants of different ages.

Two kinds of check must be made. The first is to see whether there are differences between sub-groups in terms of the range and distribution of the test scores. By way of example, assume that two clerical tests (A and B) are being tried out. The form of the trial is to administer both tests to all applicants but not to take the scores into account when making selection decisions. At the end of the trial period a simple first analysis would involve computing summary tables of test scores for each test for each sub-group of interest. In Table 4, 50 male and 50 female candidates are being compared. Both tests have a score range from 0 to 50. The distribution of scores achieved on Test A is the same for both men and women, and at this stage the test does not discriminate unfairly against members of either sex. In contrast, women have done much better on Test B, and if a single cut-off point were to be used when selecting staff, unfair discrimination could be a prob-lem. For example, if the cut-off point were to be 21, 23 men would be recruited and 37 women.

There has been speculation about whether a second kind of discrimination might arise because the effectiveness of a test might vary from group to group, and this possibility should be checked too. The possibility is illustrated in the following example involving Test A only.

Imagine that six months after giving the test to the last of the applicants in the trial, the perform-ance of the applicants is assessed and the relationship between test scores and job perform-ance is tabulated. The results are shown in Table 5.

Table 4 |

| Test score | Numbers achieving these scores | | | |
| | Test A | | Test B | |
	Male	Female	Male	Female
41–50	10	10	5	15
31–40	10	10	8	12
21–30	10	10	10	10
11–20	10	10	12	8
0–10	10	10	15	5

(Note: the range of scores achieved on a test usually approximates to the normal curve shown in Figure 2 – Tables 4 and 5 have been simplified for the purposes of illustration.)

Table 5 |

Scores on Test A	Job performance					
	Male and female combined		Male		Female	
	acceptable	unacceptable	acceptable	unacceptable	acceptable	unacceptable
41–50	16	4	7	3	9	1
31–40	14	6	6	4	8	2
21–30	12	8	5	5	7	3
11–20	10	10	6	6	6	4
0–10	8	12	6	6	4	6

For Test A, Table 4 showed no obvious unfair discrimination in the scores achieved by each sex. However, Table 5 shows a different predictive relationship between test score and job performance for men and women: a score of 11–20 indicates 60 per cent probability of acceptable job performance for women, whereas men must achieve a score of 31–40 for the probability of acceptable job performance to be at the same level.

So although an overall pass mark of 21–30 would give a 60 per cent probability of acceptable job performance, this could be viewed as discrimination against women whose chances of success would be 60 per cent with a score in the range of 11–20.

If a single cut-off is used, tests may thus discriminate unfairly against a particular sub-group because of differences in the overall distribution of test scores achieved and/or because of differences in the predictive relationship between test and job performance.

If findings of this kind arise in either case, the following issues must be considered:

- Have the numbers involved in analysis been large enough for statistically reliable conclusions to be drawn? Table 5 is based on 100 people, but when divided into 20 'cells' some of the numbers are small and none is into double figures. This is one reason why total groups of 200 or more are desirable for statistical purposes.
- Could other factors be at play? For example, in the case of clerical tests, male applicants may not have studied relevant subjects at school.
- Take other action?

Each of these points will now be considered in turn.

Sample sizes

In order to draw accurate conclusions about the occurrence of unfair discrimination, there should ideally be at least 100 people in each of the sub-groups that are of interest. However, any gross differences may be apparent from samples half that size. Although test users can often obtain adequate samples of male and female applicants, they can find it difficult to obtain sufficient numbers from different ethnic minority groups.

(This raises the separate issue of how to categorise and group such individuals for this type of analysis – a complex issue in itself.) If numbers are very small, they can sometimes be built up by reference to data collected about previous intakes of staff, to data collected for the same test by other employers, or to data collected by the test publisher. If a new and unproven test shows signs of unfair discrimination, results should not be taken into account at the time of selection and the validity of the test and the reasons for discrimination should be investigated by an expert as soon as a sufficient sample has built up.

Investigating other factors

If differences in test performance are based on substantial sample sizes, the underlying reasons should be investigated. It may be found, for example, that if previous experience (or lack of it) seems to be the reason for differences in performance, some of the effects of previous experience might be overcome by offering relevant experience prior to testing (eg a special short course).

Taking other action

The following possibilities should be considered and expert advice taken on them:

- Can an alternative test be found which is equally effective in terms of predictive validity but which does not discriminate?
- Can the test be redesigned so that those items that are discriminating unfairly are dropped?
- Can alternative tests (or even alternative methods of selection) be offered to applicants? For example, potential applicants could be sifted either by passing public or internal examinations, or by passing an aptitude test, or by attending a job-related training course.

If none of the above possibilities is feasible, the apparent conflict between the spirit and the letter of the law presents real problems for responsible employers who wish to comply with current legislation.

The dilemma is illustrated by the following example. Suppose that for several years tests have been administered to 2,000 applicants (1,000 male and 1,000 female) in order to shortlist 100 for interview, and that the same pass mark has been used for both groups. Follow-up shows that this has resulted in 70 males being called for interview and 30 females – ie 7 per cent of males and 3 per cent of females. Follow-up also shows that the test has been an effective predictor of performance, so there is reluctance to consider any of the alternatives described above.

Under these circumstances an employer who wishes to observe the spirit of the law might continue to shortlist the 7 per cent of males but to increase the number of females short-listed to 7 per cent as well. This would increase the numbers that are called for interview but would avoid the challenge that males are being disadvantaged (7 per cent would still be called for short-listing) or that females were the subject of discrimination (the percentage called forward would now be identical to that for the men).

Although such a strategy might satisfy the spirit of the law, its operation in the example given would depend on the use of lower pass marks for women. This would appear to conflict with the current legislation, which requires that all candidates taking the same procedure are treated equally. Where such conflicts are apparent in legislation it is normal for them to be resolved either by the hearing of a test case so that law can be established or by revision of the legislation.

The same principles can be followed when scrutinising for fairness among ethnic minority groups and disabled people. Remember that in order to be able to check the fairness of the tests (and the whole selection procedure) in this way, appropriate details must be collected from applicants at the time of selection.

Scrutiny for fairness should not be confined to tests. In particular, checks should be made that interviewers have received appropriate training, and their assessments should be monitored with the same rigour as for test scores. Indeed, not only should the fairness of the selection methods be checked but also that of the decision-making processes and the individual decision-makers.

Readers who wish to go into this very complex area are recommended to obtain a booklet entitled *Discriminating Fairly: A guide to fair selection* which was published jointly by the British Psychological Society and the Runnymede Trust, or one of the other specialist publications in this area.

The following issues are now considered:

- the potential financial and other benefits of testing to the employing organisation
- the costs of testing to the employing organisation
- other risks and possible costs.

POTENTIAL BENEFITS OF TESTING TO THE EMPLOYING ORGANISATION

The essential benefits of testing to the employing organisation can be considered under two broad headings: financial benefits and other benefits.

Financial benefits

The use of tests can lead to substantial financial benefits for three reasons:

- the quality of selection and hence the productivity of employees may be improved – further, there may be other benefits such as improved quality of work, reduced turnover, etc
- the cost of processing large numbers of applications can be minimised
- the costs of dealing with selection errors are avoided.

Improving the quality of selection

If the use of tests leads to better-quality staff being selected, the tests may contribute to the cost-effectiveness of selection in three ways: first, precisely because the job performance of those taken on is better; second, because those selected by the improved methods may need less training and stay longer, thus reducing the organisation's recruitment and training bills; and third, because those taken on may be more suitable than external applicants when it comes to promotion to a higher level, so that the cost of subsequent recruitment may also be reduced. However, the needs of subsequent jobs will have to be taken into account at the time of selection if this third benefit is to be achieved.

In a job where performance can be measured objectively, it is possible to calculate the actual financial savings that can be achieved by improving selection and thus increasing output or reducing the numbers of employees required to meet the output targets (Schmidt and Hunter, 1979; Hunter and Schmidt, 1982; Smith, 1986). In a paper describing assessment centres (including psychometric tests) used in the selection of senior police and prison officers, Bedford and Feltham (1986) estimated annual net savings of over £1.3 million. The technique for making these kinds of calculations is known as utility analysis, and it can be used for representing the cost-effectiveness of any selection methods. However, it is a highly technical subject beyond the scope of this book, and the reader is referred to Roth, Bobko and Mabon (2000) for a detailed treatment of the subject, and to Cooper, Robertson and Tinline (2003, pages 199–204) for a brief outline and illustration of the method.

For many management jobs it is not possible to quantify the actual savings in this way, but the financial benefit to be gained by an organisation from making a good selection decision is potentially far greater. In many cases it may not be only the salary and overheads associated with employing the individual that are at stake, but the future prospects of the company can be jeopardised if a bad decision is made in respect of a key post – one has only to recall the case of the merchant bank Barings and the damage done by one of their employees, Nick Leeson, to see this.

Minimising the cost of processing large numbers of applications

Mention has already been made of the use of tests as a way of sifting applications. The aim of sifting is to increase the final selection ratio (see Chapter 6).

Other potential benefits of testing

Monitoring and maintenance of standards

The use of tests allows benchmarking comparisons between applicants both over time and at different places. Most commercially available tests have a wide range of norms available which allow comparisons to be made with similar applications to other organisations, although such data are normally supplied in confidence by the users to the test publishers and the names of the supplying organisations may not be known to other users. Large organisations may have enough data to draw up their own comparative norms as well. The standard of individual applicants can be compared and one applicant group can be judged against another.

Attracting better applicants

There is a growing body of evidence to show that the use of systematic assessment procedures, applied in a professional manner, has an impact on candidates' perceptions of the organisation and increases their willingness to accept a job offer if one is made (Anderson, Born and Cunningham-Snell, 2001). However, although tests may contribute to this, much depends on the way they are presented to the candidate (Fletcher, 1997).

AVOIDING THE COST OF ERRORS

Apart from poor performance in terms of quantity and quality of work (which might not be confined to a individual but may also affect direct reports, a team, a section, a division or even a subsidiary company), the cost of dealing with errors in selection can be considerable. For example, training periods may be extended, additional training arranged, etc. Ultimately, there may be time required to go through dismissal procedures – and perhaps complications due to union involvement or an appeal to an employment tribunal. Also important although difficult to assess in purely financial terms are the 'human' costs, including the disappointment for those recruited who have not reached the required standard, and pressures on staff who have to manage the poor performance and dismissal processes.

Costs of testing to the employing organisation

Against the expected financial and other benefits, the potential user must set the cost of gaining access to testing expertise and introducing and sustaining a testing programme. Below, the main issues in terms of costs are summarised.

Gaining access to testing expertise

Ways of gaining access to testing expertise, and the costs involved, were described in Chapter 5.

Introducing and sustaining a testing programme

Once testing expertise is available there are four main stages in introducing and sustaining a testing programme: first, training test administrators; second, obtaining the materials; third, monitoring the programme; and fourth, reviewing the programme. Costs likely to be incurred at each of these stages are:

- training accredited testers – Training often involves residential training courses. Costs are incurred both for the registration and residential fees, and also as a result of absence from work. In Chapter 5 we gave details of costs of training – a person wishing to use a full range of tests from one supplier would cost almost £5,000 (plus VAT) in residential training fees. Because courses differ in the tests offered, training venues, etc, there can be marked differences in fees charged.

- obtaining test materials – Such a range and diversity of psychological tests are available that it is impossible to give any idea of typical costs. However, some question booklets cost around £20 to lease for a year, and some answer sheets around £5. Catalogues and price-lists are produced annually by most suppliers; current price-lists should be checked by organisations that are calculating the costs of introducing testing. At least one publisher also charges licensing fees of approximately £1,500 per test for a corporate licence fee. Although costs can be substantial, they are minor compared with the costs incurred if, for example, errors are made in the appointment of senior managers whose influence may extend well beyond their own department.

- monitoring a testing programme – Once a testing system is established, organisations should allocate resources to make sure that they are being used properly. Without such monitoring it is possible that some of those administering tests may fall into bad habits – it is surprising how many test administrators are tempted to alter the time allowed for tests, etc. However, such monitoring seldom takes place.

- reviewing a testing programme – The pace of change is such that it is increasingly common for the number and nature of jobs to have altered within a relatively short period, and this may mean a fresh approach to selection. Clearly, if new tests are thought appropriate, there may be some costs in introducing them. It is also possible for the applicant pool to change in quantity and quality – because of competition, demographic fluctuations, and so on. All in all, this can increase the costs of testing programmes because they run for a shorter time before they have to be updated and modified.

Other risks and possible costs

The main areas where costs will be incurred have now been described. However, there are also other indirect costs and risks accompanying testing which an organisation should be aware of, and consider. These are: test security, test popularity, possible adverse effects on candidates, possible outside scrutiny, and registration under the Data Protection Act.

Test security

From time to time there are reports of tests being compromised. For example, one company found its manual dexterity test – involving placing washers and nuts on to screw threads – had been studiously copied and that some applicants were attending for practice at a nearby house before going on to the company for their proper test see case study 8, page 5. Although there is nothing wrong with practice sessions *per se* – and, indeed, there is a lot to be said for them, many tests having a built-in supervised practice session (see below) – it is important in selection to treat all applicants equally. Either all applicants should have opportunities to practise for the specified and carefully timed period or no one should. Accordingly, every effort must be made to maintain test security (eg applicants should not have the opportunity to copy the test materials), and if tests are heavily used, parallel forms should be professionally developed so that applicants are unlikely to know the particular version that they are given.

Test popularity

The popularity of some commercially available tests can lead to further difficulties. For example, in graduate recruitment it is possible that the same applicant will take the same tests in several different organisations within a relatively short period, since many big companies tend to favour a rather restricted range of tests. With ability tests, this is likely to result in some applicants steadily improving their scores as they remember some 'correct' answers and thus have more time to work out answers to other questions. Much the same might be said of personality questionnaires which graduate applicants might encounter several times. If they get feedback on their score profiles, it may influence their responses to the same questionnaire subsequently.

Possible adverse effects on candidates

A potential problem in the use of tests is that some applicants may lack confidence in their own abilities and either not put themselves forward if testing is involved, or suffer from debilitating test anxiety if they do attend the selection process. The possibility of intimidation is a particular problem when dealing with less academic school-leavers, older candidates, people trying to return to work after a period of non-employment, etc. However, in order to try to overcome this problem and minimise any advantage or disadvantage to particular groups which could arise from their 'ability to take tests', many tests have example questions for candidates to do in their own time before starting the test proper. Such example questions enable the candidates to familiarise themselves with the format of the questions and reduce their fears. Another way to deal with this is to provide applicants with a handout explaining, in friendly non-technical language, why tests are being used and giving example questions (see Chapter 4). Practice items and explanatory materials should be easy to understand and thus encourage applicants; ideally candidates should be given explanations of any difficulties either in supplementary instructions or through the test administrator.

Possible outside scrutiny

At the time of writing, organisations that use tests may have to justify their actions to one of the three existing equality commissions – the Commission for Racial Equality, the Equal Opportunities Commission, and the Disability Rights Commission. Appropriate analyses were described earlier in this chapter. The Commissions may wish to look into the origins and worth of a test if a complaint about its fairness is made. However, there is no reason to think that the current commissions or the new Commission for Equality and Human Rights which may replace them in 2006 will look at a test any more than they look at any other aspect of selection procedures, including application forms and interviews. If the content of the test has been carefully matched to the requirements of the job and its use is based on past experience of the reasons for success and failure (as it should be), it is very unlikely that any of these bodies will find any reason to investigate. Nevertheless, care should be taken to ensure that tests avoid the use of colloquial English, and do not assume knowledge more likely to be known by one sex than by the other, by one racial group than by another, etc.

Registration under the Data Protection Act 1998

If test scores linked to individuals' names are to be kept on computer, it is necessary that the employing organisation registers this under the terms of the Data Protection Act. If an organisation's computer system is already registered under the Act, it should be only an administrative formality to add an extra item (ie test scores) to the specification. However, once individuals are granted rights of access to personal details that are held on computer, organisations whose systems include test scores will have to develop procedures for providing individuals with meaningful feedback about their performance and take appropriate steps regarding copyright (see Chapter 12). Raw scores alone are at best meaningless and at worst dangerous and open to misinterpretation (see Chapters 2, 7 and 8). Test results should not stay on the computer after their useful life unless they are to form part of a validation or other study (see Chapter 8). Also, steps must be taken to ensure that only accredited users have access to this information.

EVALUATING TESTS OUTSIDE THE AREA OF SELECTION

Tests can be used at work for other reasons – for example, to help people to take stock of themselves as part of their planning for future development. Tests can also be used as an aid to career choice, as an aid to fitting people into new organisational structures.

From the point of view of evaluation such situations are extremely complex. On the one hand test scores and profiles may be only a small part of the information about the individual; on the other hand the range of choices and options facing the individual are such that it is impossible to compare like with like. In particular, decisions about the future may involve issues about a partner's employment, children's schooling and the quality of life as well as cognitive skills, personality and values.

Nevertheless, some evaluation of the tests should be done, even if it is no more than asking those involved whether they feel that the tests have 'added value' to their thinking and decision-making. As the following case study shows, evaluation can sometimes have some unexpected results.

CASE STUDY 19

The evaluation of tests used for placement on a college course

A college lecturer wanted the college to do more for young people who had been unsuccessful academically at school. He decided to set up a course for these young people and to place them on other college courses as their abilities and skills became apparent.

After discussion it was agreed that those being considered for the course would be given the Differential Aptitude Test. It was felt that the contrasting tests within this test battery would help the lecturer to assess the strengths and limitations of the applicants.

The course ran for several years. Students generally developed well in terms of their self-confidence but struggled to pass the examinations at the end of the courses on which they were placed.

Analysis of the test scores showed that the scores had been very good predictors of the small number of students who had been successful in examinations and the large number who had not.

However, the college lecturer was unable to attract more able students to the course. Fearful that if he didn't take more people on to the course, the course would close, he decided that the tests should no longer form part of the selection procedure.

11

Testing in a wider context: other methods of assessment and development

Nowadays a growing number of methods other than psychometrics are used to assess and develop people's ability, aptitude, personality and motivation. These methods include psychometric instruments as an important input to the process – for example, assessment/development centres (already referred to briefly in Chapter 6 above), self-development workshops, 360-degree appraisals and team development workshops. At the heart of most of these you will find the competencies approach to identifying and assessing personal characteristics.

In this chapter we describe the competencies approach, the most common alternative methods, the role of tests within them, and their relative advantages and disadvantages.

COMPETENCIES MODELS

The competency approach was devised in the 1970s by the US consultancy company McBer to identify those personal characteristics which result in effective and/or superior performance in a job. According to Boyatzis (1982), in his book which documents the McBer work,

> *A job competency is an underlying characteristic of a person in that it may be a motive, trait, skill, aspect of one's self-image or social role, or a body of knowledge which he or she uses.*

He also introduces the important concept of the 'threshold' competency: those characteristics just mentioned which are essential to performing the job but are not causally related to superior performance. Competencies were identified using interviews incorporating the critical incident technique. However, according to Boyatzis, his study 'does not provide enough information for the development or implementation of selection or promotion systems'. This approach is often referred to as *personal competencies*, as opposed to the *occupational competencies* or Standards approach adopted in the UK since the late 1980s. The latter concentrates on the job, as opposed to the individual, and aims to specify in very detailed behavioural terms standards of performance required to carry out a job competently or effectively.

The Standards approach is used widely in the UK as an assessment tool for accrediting National Vocational Qualifications (NVQs) for a wide range of jobs from semi-skilled up to middle-management levels. The Management Charter Initiative (MCI) has produced Standards for first-level, middle and senior management levels, while the Institute of Directors and Henley Management College have produced standards for directors. However, in this chapter we concentrate on the personal competencies approach since it focuses on the individual's personal characteristics, and so is much more appropriate to assessment and development applications.

One of the first personal competency models developed in the UK was the Job Competencies Survey, now called the Personal Competencies Survey (PCS), which has evolved over the last 20 years through the work of the second author in the fields of assessment centres (ACs) and management competencies. The first version, produced in 1986, drew heavily on the literature at the time and was originally used as a questionnaire for the first stage of the job analysis process for identifying competencies of senior and middle managers in large companies such as Shell International, Barclays, British Gas and Smiths Industries. It was first used for appraisal in 1988 on the executive development workshop within the general and senior management courses at Henley Management College, and has been revised after many years of extensive applications and research in several countries.

The overall framework is extremely comprehensive, consisting as it does of 45 competencies under six main headings covering Intellectual, Personal, Communication, Interpersonal, Leadership and Results-orientation competencies. For more details of the specific competencies, see the list below. The behavioural definitions of the competencies, and information on the 360-degree appraisal procedure for which it is used are presented in the manual (Dulewicz, 1997). This model is fairly typical of the generic competency frameworks currently used in the UK.

Intellectual
1 *Information collection*
2 *Problem analysis*
3 *Numerical interpretation*
4 *Judgement*
5 *Critical faculty*
6 *Creativity*
7 *Planning*
8 *Perspective*
9 *Organisational awareness*
10 *External awareness*
11 *Learning orientation*
12 *Technical expertise*

Personal
13 *Adaptability*
14 *Independence*
15 *Integrity*
16 *Stress tolerance*

17 *Resilience*
18 *Detail-consciousness*
19 *Self-management*
20 *Change orientation*

Communication
21 *Reading*
22 *Written communication*
23 *Listening*
24 *Oral expression*
25 *Oral presentation*

Interpersonal
26 *Impact*
27 *Persuasiveness*
28 *Sensitivity*
29 *Flexibility*
30 *Ascendancy*
31 *Negotiating*

Leadership
32 *Organising*
33 *Empowering*
34 *Appraising*
35 *Motivating others*
36 *Developing others*
37 *Leading*

Results-orientation
38 *Risk-taking*
39 *Decisiveness*
40 *Business sense*
41 *Energy*
42 *Concern for excellence*
43 *Tenacity*
44 *Initiative*
45 *Customer orientation*

ASSESSMENT AND DEVELOPMENT CENTRES

The assessment centre method of identifying potential is primarily a British invention, formulated first in World War II by the armed forces in the form of the War Office Selection Board, and followed soon after by the UK Civil Service. Since then, assessment centres have been used for other purposes (see below).

The first well-documented industrial application was in the USA by the telephone company AT&T in 1955, and since then their use has mushroomed to the point that the latest estimates suggest that there are around 3,000 centres in that country alone. The picture in the UK is very similar. More than a half of medium-sized and large companies use assessment centre (AC) exercises, according to recent surveys – an example was described in Chapter 1 (case study 2).

An AC is a multifaceted, multidimensional approach to which a number of personal characteristics, or personal competencies (see above), required for successful performance at the target level or job are first identified and then assessed, using a range of situational exercises designed to simulate tasks at the target level and psychometric ability tests and personality questionnaires. The exercises are normally observed and assessed by a team of assessors specially trained for the task of systematic assessment, who make evaluations and make recommendations for potential and action plans.

A typical AC includes some or all of the following exercises:

- an *in-tray (in-basket) exercise*, which typically contains 20–35 items, nearly all of which should be based on actual items from target job-holders' in-trays, although a few can be specially designed to tie together the other items in the fictitious company on which the exercise is based – It can take up to two hours to complete, and is often followed by an interview with one of the assessors who probes the actions taken on high-priority items and also the general approach adopted

- a *leaderless group discussion* in which four to six participants normally form a committee to achieve a given objective – Often an individual is asked to support a particular course of action, and to convince his or her peers of the merits of the case

- an *assigned leader exercise*, in which participants take turns to be the leader for a specific period – A different topic or task is presented to each member of the group to tackle

- a *presentation* on a particular topic of relevance to the target job – The participants present their case individually, to one or two of the assessors. Typically, they each have around ten minutes for their presentation, followed by up to ten minutes of probing questions from the assessors

- a *written report*, also on a subject of relevance to the target job – The participants are usually asked to write a 3- or 4-page report

- a *role-play exercise*, in which the participant is typically asked to conduct a fact-finding, sales or disciplinary interview with a subordinate or customer, played by a trained member of staff.

In many centres it is common for ability tests and personality questionnaires to be administered as well. Cognitive (often verbal and numerical critical thinking) tests normally relate to the competence analysis, whereas personality questionnaire results apply to a number of the interpersonal, motivational and emotional adjustment competencies. Often, personality results are fed into the assessors' conference by a psychologist or accredited tester whenever they appear relevant to the discussion. Unless there is a significant time interval between the assessment centre and any subsequent centre or other procedures for promoting staff, the test and questionnaires used for promotion must be different from those used at the centre.

One reason ACs are so widely used for identifying potential is the number of problems found with alternative methods, such as appraisal systems or committees of wise managers. These problems often arise when the demands of more senior positions are significantly different from those of the current job – the competencies required are likely to be very different, so current performance cannot be expected to be an accurate guide to future potential. Psychological tests and questionnaires can be a valuable measure of a person's intellectual capacities, personality and motivation, but they do not always provide a comprehensive assessment of all the relevant competencies or the degree of behavioural detail often required to identify a full enough set of training and development needs.

There are two other main reasons for this trend. First, the scientific evidence: with a large-scale programme, even a small increase in validity can result in a disproportionately large increase in the net benefit derived, in performance and monetary value of staff selected. Second, numerous case studies from a range of different organisations have been published in recent years to testify to the great benefit derived by both participants and assessors from taking part in an AC, and the evidence from the vast majority of more than 50 validation studies presented in a seminal meta-analysis study (Gaugler, Rosenthal, Thornton and Bentson, 1987) indicates that ACs predict future performance or success very well – certainly better than any other widely researched assessment tool. Schmidt and Hunter (1998) also report that assessment centre scores do predict rate of promotion and advancement in management.

For many years ACs focused largely or exclusively on the assessment of potential for the next job up, or longer-term prospects over the next five years or so. These events were run primarily for the benefit of the organisations, the participant gaining little or no feedback apart from whether he or she got the job. However, over the last decade or two, the aims of many centres have switched, much greater emphasis being placed on the development of participants. Many centres nowadays combine assessment of potential with detailed feedback to participants, who get a lengthy feedback session with an assessor, culminating in an agreed action plan to help him or her address those weaknesses identified in the centre that are relevant to realising his or her full potential.

Sometimes written reports are provided for participants too. However, if such reports are to influence appointments, they will be subject to intense scrutiny by the participants and considerable care must be taken with their quality (see case study 9, page 6).

Some centres are now run purely for the benefit of the participant, who 'owns' all the data collected. Assessors – usually called observers or facilitators – provide participants with evaluations of performance and advise on interpretation and action planning. But it is the individual who is responsible for collating and interpreting the information, and for organising the follow-up action.

Whereas in the USA it is the norm not to use psychometric tests and questionnaires in ACs or development centres, in the UK they are usually incorporated, and in many events play a central role. They add invaluable information in two main ways.

First, they provide a rigorous, objective assessment of mental ability and ultimate capacity of participants which cannot always be spotted by assessors. It can be extremely valuable to know that a participant who has performed poorly in some exercises has in fact got a high level of mental ability. Such information usually stimulates a valuable debate in the assessor's conference.

Second, with personality data it is sometimes very difficult for assessors to evaluate certain competencies accurately, especially those in the emotional or motivation domains, even in a two-day event. Internal states can be assessed much more accurately and objectively by personality questionnaires (PQs), even if the data is based on self-perceptions. Once again, any differences can be fruitfully explored in the assessor's conference. So, unlike the USA where the development centres are usually seen as an alternative approach to psychometrics, in the UK tests are normally used to provide evidence which complements the assessor's judgement, and which can be particularly valuable in their own right in development centres.

A third use of assessment centres has been for the recruitment of staff. The combination of events used to select top managers (see Chapter 9) may be called an assessment centre, although the aim of the procedure is primarily to assess ability to 'hit the ground running' rather than consider future potential. Such centres often include activities closely related to elements of the work to be done, and in this way some of the events could be viewed as work samples. Given the diverse nature and purpose of assessment centres it is particularly difficult to generalise about them – however, Schmidt and Hunter (1998) report that work sample tests for trades people do add 24 per cent to the validity of selection based on general mental ability (GMA) alone.

An extensive literature exists for those who wish to study the subject in more detail. Woodruffe (2000) provides a very comprehensive overview. For details of setting up and running assessment and development centres, and for relating them to competency frameworks, see Dulewicz (1989; 1991).

SELF- AND TEAM DEVELOPMENT WORKSHOPS

Self-development workshops are often used as an alternative to an assessment/development centre (ADC), and have been described as 'ADCs without the situational exercises'. They depend heavily on psychometric and other instruments that are usually completed by participants, their bosses, their subordinates and other staff – a 360-degree appraisal (see below). Self-development workshops normally address not only competencies but also personality, leadership style, stress, attitudes, career anchors and aspirations, and motivation. The workshop leader often provides a theoretical input on these matters, and then guides participants through the interpretation of their scores. Sharing results and discussion among participants is also usually encouraged. The end result is an action plan that members pursue back on the job, often under the guidance of a mentor (also see 'Development workshops', Chapter 9).

Team-building workshops are a variant of self-development workshops in which established or new teams are assembled in order to develop their group process and working procedures. Teams usually work under the guidance of a facilitator who instructs them on the nature of group process and working procedures, and shows them how to develop their own methods, tailored to the needs of their team, and how to improve team performance. Both practical and cerebral exercises are the main vehicles used, but personality questionnaires often provide an invaluable input, since questionnaires such as 16PF^R and OPQ^R produce 'second-order' factor scores on highly relevant constructs such as team roles, leadership style and follower style. Such data can be invaluable for informing members about the composition of the team, for helping teams to understand why they are performing below their best, and sometimes for giving an indication of how members might develop both as an individual and as a team member.

360-DEGREE APPRAISAL

In contrast to ADCs and development workshops in which, as just noted, psychometrics have an important role, the 360-degree appraisal approach is used nowadays by many organisations as an alternative to ability and personality testing. In this section we provide an overview of the process.

Questionnaires have been used as a vital tool in appraisal and job analysis for over 50 years, but there has been a major growth in their use in recent years. In appraisal, the emphasis has traditionally been on the annual review by the boss, with the results determining pay increases. Research has shown, however, that this process has done little for the development of staff and often sets the wrong climate for that. Other processes have therefore evolved to achieve this end. There has also been a change in the focus of appraisal, and the factors under review, with the dramatic growth in the use of competencies since the early 1980s when, as just mentioned, the US consultancy McBer first pioneered this approach. In addition, with the trend towards flatter organisations, teamworking and greater openness and involvement, we have seen a shift away from solo appraisal by the boss towards multiple appraisal by all who have contact with the employee – even subordinates and customers. To capture the flavour of this all-round view, the process has become known as 360-degree appraisal.

A 360-degree appraisal process gathers ratings of participants' current performance on each competence from themselves and from other people who know them well, against the standards expected at their level in the organisation. These 'self' and 'other' ratings of current proficiency provide views from different vantage-points. The views may not all be exactly the same because these other people will probably have seen participants working in different situations, and so have seen different facets of their performance. There is also inevitably a degree of subjectivity in these ratings. Notwithstanding, these views provide a detailed and comprehensive picture of current performance, and participants are encouraged to stand back and identify the true picture that should emerge.

All the information gathered about the present and future importance of the various competencies, and the ratings of performance, are usually brought together in a report. A typical report covers:

- definitions of the competencies appraised
- the competencies that are important
- a summary and overview of performance
- a detailed analysis of performance, covering strengths. development needs, growth needs and under-utilised potential
- action planning.

In their report, participants are normally encouraged to draw up action plans to enable them to maximise their learning opportunities. Participants are often advised to find a facilitator – an individual with great experience of personal development – to help with this difficult but important task. Inputs on key issues relating to human abilities, personality, motivation, attitudes and other relevant subjects should also be sought from their facilitator to help with the action planning.

OTHER SELECTION METHODS

Other selection methods and criteria include structured interviews, job knowledge tests, the evaluation of previous training and experience, reference checks, years of previous experience, biographical data measures, length of education, and interests. Numerical values can be assigned to all this information so that statistical analyses can be carried out. Schmidt and Hunter (1998) have drawn together the research findings about all these methods and have reported on the extent to which they add to predictions made from a test of general mental ability (GMA) used on its own.

RELATIVE ADVANTAGES AND DISADVANTAGES OF TESTS

Tests have been the most widely used scientific assessment tool for almost 100 years. As we have seen above, this is largely because:

- they are derived from well-researched models in the scientific literature
- the constructs measured are clearly defined
- results are standardised so objective users must be well-trained, and
- accredited validation studies have demonstrated their value for predicting future performance.

Rigour and validity are the main reasons why tests are used both in isolation and as an important and integral part of other methods just described. Their main disadvantages appear to be that:

- they are based almost exclusively on self-report, although at least one personality questionnaire invites rating from colleagues
- they do not provide the degree of detailed, relevant and comprehensive behavioural

data generated by ADCs and by 360-degree appraisals. This type of output can be so valuable when drawing up action plans from these methods

- they must be administered and interpreted by qualified users and materials are restricted – true tests cannot, for example, be sent out by post or via the Internet to people not trained in their use. Unfortunately, these positive features can add significantly to the cost, and so to the attractiveness of some other methods.

Although the validity of ability tests is almost universally accepted, doubts still linger in some quarters about personality questionnaires because of a few articles, some highly misleading, in the press a few years ago.

Many users find other methods attractive because of these disadvantages of tests. However, the competency and 360-degree approaches also have advantages and disadvantages. The advantages include a wide range of job-related behaviours. The disadvantages include the issue of deciding which behaviours (or competencies) are required in specific jobs – there is the danger of looking at the obvious or stereotyped behaviours rather than the underlying behaviours and skills. A further issue is to find ways of describing standards of, for example, creativity in ways in which people can accurately assess themselves and others.

The validity of a well-designed ADC used for long-term development is, however, even higher than for tests, or any other *single* method, primarily because it gets the best of all worlds by incorporating several different methods, including tests. Most self- and team development workshops are only as valid as the tests used within them. And the case for 360-degree appraisal, in terms of its scientific properties, has yet to be fully established. It has many positive features, especially its comprehensiveness in terms of the use of multiple raters (although as noted, this can also cause problems), and the wide range of relevant competencies which can be assessed, but the approach is relatively new and unproven compared to psychological tests which have been in use for about 100 years.

12

Testing on the Internet, and other developments

This final chapter has been prepared with the help of representatives of leading UK test publishers: their details are given in the Acknowledgements section at the start of the book. There is no easy way of summarising the contents of this chapter. On the one hand, tests appear to be widely accepted at present, and the issue uppermost in the minds of some users is how to reduce time and costs. On the other hand, there is concern that the demand for efficiency may lead to a number of problems for individuals and for organisations, and that these in turn may lead to legislation that either aims to improve quality standards and/or restricts the use of tests. We begin by considering the impact of testing on the Internet and the many other changes arising from the use of computer technology: our framework is that of the book as a whole. We then look at other developments which do not involve computers and the Internet and consider in turn

- how tests are used
- trends in the types of tests and questionnaires available
- possible changes in legislation affecting testing, and the role of the British Psychological Society
- changes in preparation for testing
- the use of testing as part of advanced selection methods.

After our concluding comments we end by reminding readers of ways in which they can keep informed about current developments.

THE IMPACT OF TESTING ON THE INTERNET

The most significant development in testing over the last five years has been the use of the Internet. As noted in Chapter 4, there seems to be a high demand for Internet testing among HR professionals. The *People Management* (2001) survey found that 'more than three quarters of the HR professionals want the [online testing] service'. And a CIPD recruitment survey (Czerny, 2004) showed that 'the use of online testing is growing, with 6.9 per cent of organisations using some kind of online testing in 2003, compared to 0.9 per cent in 2002'. This is presumably because it has a number of important advantages:

- Access to test users and takers is worldwide. Anyone with a PC linked to the Internet can sit a test, the results can be processed almost instantly, and a report can be produced and sent to users or test-takers within a few minutes.

- Publishers can use the data gathered for conducting further development work and research on their instruments in order to improve them and demonstrate their effectiveness.

- Test results can be used by companies for screening applicants for jobs in order to reduce large applicant pools quickly and effectively.

- The Internet could also significantly increase the number of people who take tests for self-development purposes, and dramatically reduce the costs.

These are just a few of the potential benefits claimed by advocates of Internet testing, and the major test producers are responding to demand.

In 2001 Professor Dave Bartram, R&D Director of SHL, stated that his company launched its first web-based service recently and reported that clients were already seeing benefits in terms of time and cost of recruitment. However, other publishers are being more cautious. In the same year, Dr Robert McHenry, chairman of OPP, another major test publisher, argued against firms conducting tests online, and warned practitioners against buying into the promise that testing will be easier, cheaper and more convenient when it comes to remote candidates. At the moment, there is a difference between the promise and the reality. 'Existing Internet test sites are not as convenient as you would have thought.' OPP is developing a system – to be released in 2005 – that will allow managers to assess candidates using a combination of computer-based and telephone tests. It will be based on software sent via email.

The Internet can obviously provide the user with many worthwhile benefits, but unless the conventional standards of control and supervision are retained, there is a clear danger that we will throw out the baby with the bathwater. Hitherto reputable tests could easily become debased as they enter the public domain and professional standards decline. They would eventually become indistinguishable from all the other Mickey Mouse tests on the Internet, and consequently both test-users and -takers would lose out in the long run. Furthermore, a number of ethical concerns about the use of personal test data and reports must be addressed and resolved.

The main application of Internet testing currently is for graduate recruitment. Most large and medium-sized companies are using tests and competencies questionnaires for screening out large numbers of applicants. Because they can have up to 10,000 applicants, one can see the attractions – but there have been concerns raised about unprofessional or expedient practices. In a paper at the BPS Conference on Testing in 2003, a presenter reported how one company's online tests results did not produce the expected normal distribution of scores. He admitted that chosen candidates had to obtain the maximum score on a numerical test, which placed them at the 90th percentile. Many occupational psychologists would see the benefit in screening out the bottom 10 per cent of candidates on a *valid* test, but to screen out 90 per cent smacks of organisational expediency – it costs nothing to keep on increasing the cut-off score in order to reject more and more applicants. When an online ability test is used to reduce the application pool to the top 10 per cent of mental ability scores, candidates with a number of other, perhaps more important, social and emotional competencies and abilities could well be rejected in the process.

In addition, companies accept that there is quite a high level of cheating by candidates taking online tests. At the 2003 BPS Test Conference, one company admitted that many candidates did not pass without help. Some get another person with proven high ability to take the verbal or numerical test for them; some take the test as many times as they wish for practice (recruiters admit that Harry Potter is their most frequent applicant); and others get together in groups to take the test. Do organisations really want to have a significant number of cheats in their final applicant pools?

Furthermore, good testing practice requires all candidates to receive feedback – yet this rarely seems to happen with online testing. The normal feedback is 'You have passed/failed', even if many have achieved quite high scores. Most, if not all, graduates will get far more rejections than acceptances, and consequently their self-esteem is likely to be deflated, if not totally undermined, and at such a critical time in their studies. Dulewicz (2004) provides a wider critique of online graduate recruitment. On the wider front, Internet testing has many advantages for assessment and development purposes, but as with all goods and services, *Caveat emptor* applies – particularly so in this area.

THE IMPACT OF COMPUTER TECHNOLOGY ON TESTING

In addition to the Internet, computer technology continues to bring advances to testing by providing new methods of administering, scoring, and interpreting tests and monitoring testing programmes. It also provides new ways of testing and of test development. Each area of innovation is separate, but once access to a computer is available, changes are likely to take place in several areas. Areas of innovation are now discussed in turn, detailing first the potential benefits and then the possible disadvantages.

Test choice

Through the Internet it is possible to get access to some test and questionnaire manuals and other detailed information to help decide which might be used in a particular application. This is particularly helpful for those who are able to understand the statistical and other technical qualities of tests through attendance at Level A or Level B courses in testing or in other ways. In particular, the British Psychological Society now has the online Psychological Testing Centre (www.psychtesting.org.uk), which aims to provide impartial information about tests.

Test administration

The use of computers to administer tests offers many potential advantages over tests in a pencil-and-paper form. For example, a wider variety of test content can be used, particularly those involving perceptual tasks and response times.

The distribution of test material may be simplified if testing continues to be carried out at several locations. Instead of sending out question booklets, answer sheets, etc, there are now a number of ways of distributing the tests including (a) the use of floppy disks or CD-ROMs,

(b) refreshing existing disks by the use of additional codes supplied over the telephone, and (c) testing over the Internet. With increased access to the Internet, it is likely that the majority of the UK working population could be tested at home, although the circumstances in which some individuals might be taking the tests are likely to fall far short of professionally accepted standards.

A major recent innovation in conventional testing has been in what is called 'adaptive testing', in which a software package tailors a test to each respondent by generating new sets of questions based upon previous answers to an initial standard set. Those taking the test can, on the basis of the speed and correctness of response, be moved through the test to those items for which their chances of success are close to 50 per cent. This has the advantage of making testing sessions much shorter, and the system can vary the set of questions given to individuals who have taken the test before – a major advantage in graduate recruitment where applicants can find themselves given the same test on numerous occasions. Many large organisations are using adaptive tests for screening candidates via the Internet.

It is clear that there are many advantages to computer administration. In particular, test publishers told us of the strong demand from customers to minimise both time and cost. However, there are some disadvantages:

- The lack of personal contact and interest that a test administrator can give may mean that some candidates lose interest or concentration.

- A test has to be designed (or redesigned) for computer administration. If a computerised version of a test does not exist, programming expertise will be involved. Further, it must not be assumed that results from a pencil-and-paper test and a version of the test which is computer-administered are directly comparable because, for example, there may not be the same opportunity for the candidate to ask questions of the administrators. Even if changes have been kept to a minimum, the effect of relatively subtle changes may be important. For example, on a pencil-and-paper test, candidates may mark questions about which they are uncertain and return to them after they have attempted all the other items. The facility to mark and go back to questions in a computerised version of the test may not be available. Accordingly, different norms and cut-offs may have to be developed and used according to whether candidates have taken the pencil-and-paper or computerised versions of a test.

- The initial finance required for computerised testing can be high, particularly if large groups of candidates are to be tested at the same time and large numbers of computers or terminals are therefore required. However, tests seldom make significant demands on the computer disk space or memory, and the price of PCs is now relatively low.

- A fourth problem with computerised administration concerns the storage of responses. Under the UK Data Protection Act, individuals are entitled to a copy of the information stored about them on computer. To protect copyright, they may be denied access to any records of their replies to individual questions, but once the replies have been scored it would seem appropriate to allow access to at least the total scores on tests or sub-tests. Precisely what applicants can demand will, no doubt, be established in due course by test cases in the courts of law.

- Finally, it is possible that the results of adaptive or tailored testing could also be challenged legally because applicants are not being given identical tests. At one stage such a challenge was thought unlikely in the USA because of the familiarity of the judges, prosecutors and defendants with the principle of test design and with the Standards for Educational and Psychological Testing that were published by three eminent US organisations including the American Psychological Association. However, such testing has now been challenged in at least one US state. It remains to be seen whether adaptive testing will be challenged in the UK.

If there are a number of stages in a recruitment process involving different locations, different administrative staff, etc, there is an increased risk of impersonation so that the person being assessed at one or more of the recruitment stages is not the person actually hired. Although evidence of identity can be checked at each stage by means of documents such as passports or new-style UK driving licences, some experts believe that any testing at remote locations should be repeated during the final selection process where the candidates will be seen by the people they will be working for.

Preparation for testing

Computers and the Internet can be used to give information about careers and about the selection procedures for them, and can help them to decide whether they are ready to apply. An example is the Civil Service Fast-Stream Self-Assessment website which gives potential applicants details of the kinds of vacancies that the scheme is designed to fill and the opportunity to take the kinds of tests that are used in the assessment process. Feedback on performance is offered so that people can decide whether they are ready to make a formal application.

Scoring

Computers can score tests at very high speed, and this is nearly always done if the test has also been administered on a computer. For tests that are administered in a pencil-and-paper forms, special answer sheets can be designed which can be fed into a document reader so that responses on the answer sheets can be transferred directly into a computer. However, although this technology works well if standard answer sheets can be adapted, the technology itself and the instructions to candidates can take some fine-tuning, and users should not assume that perfect results will be obtained first time.

Interpretation

The major development in recent years has been the use of computer-generated reports on test results (usually personality) produced by 'expert systems'. They not only report on the score on each scale or dimension but also assess the total picture of personality that is being given in the way that a trained and experienced assessor may look for patterns which support each other, patterns which conflict, and so on. But even then, some psychologists are of the view that personality questionnaire results are best used as a starting point for possible lines of enquiry and discussion during an interview rather than regarded as a firm and permanent picture of personality. Such psychologists would argue that even if a full print-out is available, it is best restricted to experienced assessors able to interpret the questionnaire without the computer interpretation. In this way the print-out becomes a possible short cut to an assessment rather than a blind act of faith.

In fact, the majority of computer-generated reports or narratives are actually rather simple affairs where the program simply prints out a couple of descriptive statements in relation to each trait according to whether the individual has scored high, medium or low on it. Although these may be organised together under broader headings that they might relate to, computer programs are rarely designed to cope with or comment on combinations of scores. For example, they would not normally spell out the different behavioural implications of someone who has a high score on impulsiveness and spontaneity as well as a high score on aggression compared to someone with a low score on impulsiveness and a high degree of personal control as well as the high score on aggression. This kind of simple computer-based system – and it probably represents the majority – is thus quite crude and does not offer a very fine-grained analysis and interpretation, even though the print-outs may look quite sophisticated at first glance.

Finally, a criticism of a different kind arose in our interviews with test publishers. One repeated a claim that we have heard elsewhere – that some expert systems describe differences that are not important in ways that emphasise them. This is in response to customer feedback demanding more 'colour' in the reports.

NON-COMPUTER DEVELOPMENTS
Trends in how tests are used

We gave examples of how tests are used in Chapter 1. Although there appear to be fewer new cognitive ability tests being produced, there is every indication that they are becoming more and not less influential in assessment decision-making. One might reasonably surmise that some recent changes and outputs from the educational system are responsible for the even greater reliance being put on these measures.

Steadily improving GCSE and A-level results, greater numbers of students going to university and higher proportions of them gaining 'good' degrees have led to uncertainty in some employers' minds about whether standards are genuinely higher or assessment standards lower. Either way, if a higher proportion of students get higher grades, then higher grades may become less effective as a way of differentiating between them – leading to a search for other, additional ways of assessing intellectual capacity. Given all this, it is no surprise if some employers place more trust in cognitive ability test results.

Further, at the time of writing, concern about standards has increased with newspaper reports that an Internet company is providing A-level students with tailor-made coursework that is written for them by undergraduates.

Recently, tests have started to be used as part of university admission procedures. In the light of 81,000 applications for just 13,000 places on UK university law courses, eight law departments had agreed on a two-hour examination aimed at testing understanding of English 'because A-levels no longer provide an accurate test of ability'. In the National Admissions Test for Law, 'students will have to show that they can analyse passages and make logical deductions' by answering 40 multiple-choice questions. There will also be an essay. The plans follow the decision of Oxford, Cambridge and University College London, to introduce testing for medical students. The first biomedical Admissions Test was taken in Autumn 2003.

At the time of writing, a working party under Professor Steven Schwartz that has been reviewing 'Fair Admissions to Higher Education' has just published its *Draft Recommendations for Consultation* (www.admissions-review.org.uk). Each year 460,000 seek admission to higher education in the UK. The working party is sympathetic to the 'greater co-ordination of common tests' of the kind described in the preceding paragraph, and

> *welcomes proposals for an operational pilot of US-style SATs as a potential common test in the UK, and would welcome the evaluation of other tests with this in mind.*

As far as graduates are concerned, there are several issues. The first is to do with whether people really have completed a recognised degree course. Apart from totally fraudulent claims (said in one newspaper report to be as high as 20 per cent in South Africa) and degrees issued by organisations that are not recognised universities, one British university is said to have lost control of the validation service supporting its degrees, which were on sale at Israeli petrol stations. For those who have obtained degrees there remains the issue of whether the coursework was their own work or copied from the Internet or other sources. There is also the matter of grades. With UK government plans for up to half the population to attend university, there remains the traditional five-grade assessment system (first, upper second, lower second, and third with honours, and pass without honours), which means that the numbers within each grade are now very large indeed. The following report appeared in the *Echo*, a regional newspaper, on Monday 5 July 2004:

DEGREE SCAM 'A THREAT TO EDUCATION'

Fake degrees, GCSEs and A-levels for sale on the Internet undermine Britain's education system, an MP warned today.

Labour MP Barry Sheerman, chairman of the Commons Education Committee, said he would urge Education Secretary Charles Clarke to investigate when he comes before the Committee next week.

The move follows reports in a national newspaper that a British website is offering bogus qualifications which appear to be from genuine academic institutions for £165 a time.

Later the same month, national newspapers reported government plans to create a new category of university established by private companies or public bodies engaged heavily in training. Although it was said that teaching standards in the new universities would be closely monitored, concern was expressed about the maintenance of standards. The next day one newspaper reported a survey of university vice-chancellors that had found that '48 per cent of universities were providing special lessons in literacy and numeracy for first-year students'.

Although the survey was carried out by a political party rather than a research or academic institution, it raises further questions about what skills and abilities can be assumed in a graduate.

Add to this the need for employers to assess applicants educated in the EEC, and for all these reasons we think that the use of cognitive tests will increase as employers and others want to check the underlying abilities of those who claim public examination certificates, or who produce unfamiliar certificates from organisations unknown to them. Of course, if tests are used in this way at remote locations (eg as part of an overseas recruitment programme), it is important to check that they are administered properly (eg time limits are not exceeded) and that the person being tested really is the person being taken on. Some have expressed the view that the only way of making sure that this is the case is to retest all those tested at remote locations when they are called to the next stage in the procedure.

CASE STUDY 20

Possible impersonation

In one large UK organisation, all employees had to reach an acceptable standard on entrance tests in order to be appointed.

When one employee was dismissed for dishonesty, he claimed that he had not been able to do the work because of problems with reading and writing. However, it was clear that these problems would have meant that he would not have been able to reach the required standard on the selection test.

One possibility was that the dismissed employee had got someone to impersonate him for at least the testing part of the selection procedure. However, there had been no previous incidents of this kind, and a senior manager took the view that the cost of taking preventative measures would be greater than the costs of an occasional dismissal.

Trends in *types* of measures available and used

In our view the vast majority of new psychometric instruments being produced are personality measures. These not only include updates and revisions of well-established questionnaires, but also completely new omnibus measures of personality (ie questionnaires yielding scores on a whole range of personality traits). This suggests that 'attacks' on the use of such measures have had absolutely no impact. Although this continued growth is largely a reflection of demand, it is also stimulated in part by academic research showing some consensus on what are the main and most consistent features of personality that we should be concentrating on. These are the so-called 'Big Five' personality traits (extraversion, neuroticism, openness to experience, conscientiousness, and agreeableness) and their component elements. Of these, conscientiousness does seem particularly important in predicting success in work settings; it is also related to the assessment of integrity.

Apart from these general personality measures, new assessment instruments do seem to focus on a few popular themes. Leadership is currently a 'hot topic' within organisations and business schools. New psychometrically based leadership questionnaires have recently been developed, often originating from Bass's Transformational-Transactional model. Examples of such questionnaires include the Alimo-Metcalfe Transformational Leadership Questionnaire and Dulewicz and Higgs's Leadership Dimensions Questionnaire, which produces three different style profiles derived from transformational, transactional and involving leadership models. It then links these to a measure of the organisational context to produce advice on the most appropriate style for the situation. As noted in Chapter 3, emotional intelligence is another 'hot topic', and several questionnaires have been produced recently to provide measures of this construct.

Two other new types of measure being used are worth mentioning: questionnaires to assess teamworking and organisational culture. To some extent these are of course related and reflect a desire to go beyond the individual and to direct psychometric measurement to wider issues in organisational effectiveness. Team role measures are naturally not new, but new ones are appearing, often with a wider developmental focus. Measures of organisational climate and commitment are more widely used for assessing employee attitudes as a barometer of reactions to change, diagnosing internal problems, and so on. Research shows that they can accurately reflect differences between organisations in terms of the effectiveness of their HR systems (Fletcher and Williams, 1996; Audit Commission, 1995).

Representatives of test publishers have speculated about future requirements of testing and possible new tests. One has commented on the use of a range of test and questionnaires to help assess whether individuals might 'fit' organisations as well as specific vacancies – for example, some organisations experience a high rate of turnover among graduates because this is their first experience of permanent employment. Another comment was about identifying future leaders. There were also comments about whether tests might be used to identify those best suited to home-working, or whether tests might be designed to help with the development of home-workers. This might include testing to gain an understanding of the kinds of materials from which home-workers might best learn, and tests to check that people are actually learning while receiving training at remote locations. Tests were also seen as a way of increasing diversity and inclusiveness when selecting students for university courses (as abovementioned).

Ethical, legal and social trends

Much of the relevant UK legislation has been described earlier in the book (see Chapter 4), including the one major development since the Second Edition – namely the Disability Discrimination Act 1995. On 29 October 2003 the UK government announced that there will be a new commission, provisionally called the Commission for Equality and Human Rights (CEHR), to bring together the work of three existing commissions (the Commission for Racial Equality, the Equal Opportunities Commission and the Disability Rights Commission). Bartram (1995) has commented that the legislation dealing with unfair discrimination on grounds of race or gender has been invoked more often in the testing field, and in our view this is likely to continue.

There is also the possibility of legislation on age discrimination at some future date. One test publisher told us that some tests are unlikely to be passed by anyone over the age of 55 years. It has long been known that scores on many tests do vary with age to a limited extent – but so does job performance! Another test publisher reminded us that the way personality is expressed varies with age, and saw the need to develop both 'phenotype' questionnaires (aimed at measuring behaviour) and 'genotype' questionnaires (aimed at measuring qualities with genetic origins).

In our view the influence of European Union legislation could well increase, and have ramifications that are as yet unclear. One reason is that membership of the European Community encourages the free movement of labour within the Union. If workers from other EU countries are required to take tests, such testing may be seen as acting as a barrier to the free movement of labour within the EU, and accordingly fall foul of EU law.

A second reason is that there is a tendency to harmonise legislation within Europe, and at the moment attitudes and laws vary from one EU country to another. We were told of a number of differences. For example, we understand there is already legislation against age discrimination in Ireland. It was said that in Germany there is relatively little testing because the Works Councils tend to be against it – this is because past testing has been associated with legal cases, such as trying to show that someone injured in an accident has had a predisposition to having accidents. We have also been told that there is relatively little testing in Italy and in Spain, whereas in Scandinavia tests tend to be used primarily for developmental purposes.

A third reason is that some online test administration services originate outside the UK and the wider EU. In the future, legislators may try to insist that the relevant laws should be those that apply to where the candidate is located when taking the test, rather than the country of origin of the test or the computer server from which it is being administered. Finally, one test publisher's representative drew our attention to the fact that none of the legislation concerns the fundamental issue of whether the test (or other selection method) actually works!

Trends in the availability of tests

One issue of availability arises from the fact that recruitment and development systems are increasingly obtained as 'packages' or even outsourced. In our interviews we were told that those designing packages or bidding to do outsourced work had been approaching some major test publishers with the aim of including their tests in the publishers' packages. A number of publishers told us that they had refused because they felt that they could not be sure that the tests would be used to accepted professional standards. Some went on express concern that such 'packaging' and 'outsourcing' may lead to a drop in professional standards because the tests being offered may not be designed to the highest standards, because the quality of training in administration and interpretation may be relaxed, and because follow-up and evaluation may not take place. One said that the demand for training was falling because more companies are arranging testing over the Internet and then using reports generated by expert systems, perhaps with associated interview questions that are also computer-generated. In this way the whole recruitment process might be carried out by a line manager and there would be no involvement of occupational psychologists, HR managers or others trained in the use of tests.

Others saw new tests being introduced in response to new topics in the psychological or management literature, even though existing tests might have scales that provide good insight into these issues. Another view was that tests were sometimes used unnecessarily by people who wanted to justify their training in testing and/or sustain their personal interest in the topic.

The final availability issues arose over the issue of Level A and Level B qualifications. One test publisher suggested that the training was too academic, while others raised the issue of whether standards are stringent enough. From our own experiences, we share the latter concern. One felt that bad practice would eventually cause the bubble to burst! The related issue is whether the qualification should be issued for life, or whether there should be mandatory continuing professional development or even the need for requalification after a period of time (say, five to ten years).

Trends in the acceptability of testing

Although the use of tests for selection and other purposes is widespread and the signs are that it is continuing to grow, there is a significant minority of people who do not find testing acceptable. One such person told one of us that he had been tested at his place of employment and had then been told that he was not suited to the work that he was doing. Clearly, he felt differently, and the experience had left him angry and critical of testing (rather than of his employers and the person who had interpreted the tests in this way).

People sometimes feel that their test and questionnaire replies have particular influence on the outcome of the selection procedures' performance, and in particular can feel that they have 'failed' a reasoning test because they have not completed all the items. It is not uncommon to receive around 80 applications for one top management post, so the vast majority of people are experiencing repeated rejection. If this is not handled well, components of assessment such as testing are likely to face increasing criticism (see also the section on cost-effectiveness, below).

Trends in preparation for testing

In our view, good testing does involve letting candidates know what to expect so that they can prepare for it or even decide to withdraw their application. One of the major changes since the First Edition of this book has been the amount of advice being offered on how to prepare for tests. Information is now readily available in the form of books and other printed material, and also online from careers services and others offering careers advice. As well as advice on how to prepare for testing, there are often opportunities to take sample tests and get feedback on the results.

The Civil Service Fast-Stream Self-Assessment website was described earlier in this chapter. A second example concerns the General Management Admission Test (GMAT), a standardised test used by graduate business schools to evaluate candidates. There are three sections:

- an analytical writing assessment (two essays to be typed into the computer – one the analysis of an issue, the other an analysis of an argument)
- a quantitative section (multiple-choice questions involving problem-solving and data sufficiency)
- a verbal section (sentence correction, critical reasoning and reading comprehension).

More than 1,000 MBA programmes around the world require their applicants to submit GMAT scores in order to be considered for admission, and on the Internet a variety of fee-paying services can be found, each offering the individuals the prospect of achieving the highest possible score. Preparation methods include textbooks, residential courses, etc.

In theory, access to the preparation is open to all, and one test publisher's representative commented that some candidates were taking time to find out how they came across to others before completing personality questionnaires. But in practice it is the better informed, the better off and the better motivated who are likely to put time and perhaps money into this preparation. And although it could be argued that some of the qualities required in successful preparation are also required to study under intense pressure on a graduate business school programme, the results of such tests may reflect preparation as much as they reflect potential.

Indeed, it is interesting to reflect on the fact that one of the initial attractions of testing for organisations such as the Civil Service was that it gave an opportunity for the less well educated to show their potential. Because of the growth of the 'test coaching industry', this attraction is being lost. It is for this reason that some people argue that brief test description handouts are not enough and that organisations committed to equal opportunities should provide facilities to help people with at least the initial stages of their personal development. Others have suggested that greater use should be made of non-verbal tests that may be closer to reflecting 'true' ability rather than learned performance.

Test security

We commented on the need for test security in Chapter 7. One test publisher said 'Even now I don't think that tests used on the Internet are sufficiently robust in their design to maintain accuracy and to prevent fraud or copying.' Another expressed concern about the security of 'trade tests'. A third was anxious about the information obtained from the candidates and whether the information might find its way into the hands of third parties.

The importance of test security must be stressed. It is one thing for an HR manager to learn (as the result of using a personality questionnaire) that an individual feels that he or she lacks persuasive and assertive qualities. However, if that information was to become known outside the organisation, the individual might well be plagued by calls from unscrupulous salespeople. For this reason we would advise people not to respond to 'free' personality questionnaires – some may be designed to gain access to personal information that could then be used for commercial exploitation.

Cost-effectiveness

It can be argued that what ultimately matters is the overall cost-effectiveness of the recruitment system. Although the cost of setting up systems involving computers is high, once they are in place they can be used to collect a considerable amount of information on which 'screening' can be based to decide if the candidate should go to the next stage of the procedure. This means that those candidates invited to the final stages of selection (which tend to be the most expensive) are of a high standard, and the proportion of job offers made and accepted is high. In this way the capital and other costs can be covered. But recruiters should not lose sight of the time candidates spend or of the deflated self-esteem that many experience after repeated rejections. It is in their own longer-term self-interest to empathise more with rejected applicants since many are or will become stakeholders in the companies (ie potential customers, shareholders, suppliers).

THE INCREASED USE OF ADVANCED SELECTION METHODS

Although the UK went through a major recession in the early 1990s and 2000s, there has been little sign of a reduction in the use of psychometric testing. All the surveys show not only that test use has increased but that actual product range has increased significantly: there is a seemingly never-ending stream of new psychological tests coming on to the market. The same pattern is visible in much of the rest of Europe, although perhaps a year or two behind the UK position. More recently, the rate of growth seems to have slowed a little. To some extent this is perhaps inevitable, but it is also due to concerns over possible legal challenges to test use, as mentioned previously. One other factor is the growth in popularity of so-called 360-degree feedback systems mentioned in Chapter 11. In a developmental context, these are sometimes seen as alternatives to psychometric tests, although in reality they produce a different kind of information. Despite this slight tailing-off of the growth curve, personality measures seem to be used by around 65–70 per cent of the major employing organisations, the equivalent figures for cognitive tests and assessment/development centres being 70–75 per cent and 55–60 per cent respectively.

Tests are increasingly related to assessment couched in the terminology of company competency frameworks. This is not at all straightforward, though. The cause of the difficulty is that competency frameworks and psychological test dimensions usually describe behaviour at different levels. An individual competency description typically focuses on a broad pattern of surface behaviour relating to some aspect of work performance – eg organisation and planning. This is then described in terms of positive and negative behaviours like 'Can link own plans with wider strategic objectives', 'Prioritises demands made on his/her time', 'Carefully monitors progress', 'Initiates action without thinking it through' (all these are taken from actual examples of descriptors for such a competency). When the psychologist looks at this range of behaviour, several different psychological constructs are likely to seem relevant – thoughtfulness, analytical thinking, caution, impulsiveness, and so on. In other words, the psychological dimensions are often much narrower in nature, and several different ones may be relevant to any one competency. Even with very work-focused personality measures, such as the OPQ, this remains true.

So it becomes quite complicated to line up the psychological test dimensions with the competencies. In a few cases, there are actually no very clear or close relationships between the two. Competencies that revolve around the notion of business sense or business awareness often come into this category. More usually, though, a number of psychological constructs look to be relevant to each competency. This may raise a problem in that it is common to find that no single psychometric test fits the bill – no one of them offers measures of all the psychological dimensions that the analysis of the competency framework throws up. This being the case, the choice is either to use a lot of different tests – not attractive in terms of time or cost – or to decide to prioritise and perhaps use just one or two tests that cover most of what you are interested in. The latter is normally the course adopted.

A second, tougher, issue can arise if the psychological analysis of what is involved in the competencies suggests that the competencies do not make psychological sense. Either the psychological qualities required for different behaviours described under a single competency conflict with each other, or the same thing is true across two (or more) different competencies, implying that it is unlikely that an individual could be high on both. By way of illustration, take a competency called 'achievement orientation' for which the behavioural descriptions frequently include such things as 'Sets targets beyond those required', and 'Wants to be the best'. The psychological profile for individuals with very strong achievement motivation is not always one that fits very comfortably with the teamwork and interpersonal competencies, which often emphasise the capacity to put personal credit to one side in favour of the team, or imply giving higher priority to team cohesion and individual well-being than to personal goals.

Finally, a third possible problem stems from almost the opposite phenomenon – namely the same psychological factors contributing to different competencies. A common example would be a trait like 'emotional control' contributing to the assessment of competencies such as customer relations, resilience, interpersonal sensitivity, and so on. Having the same psychological factors relating to different competencies can cause problems in being able to discriminate between the latter and to assess them independently.

It seems that tests do not translate into competencies all that easily. Sometimes the problem lies in the quality of the original work done in identifying the competencies. But in other cases it goes deeper, and reflects an unrealistic expectation of what people can achieve. The underlying assumption of some frameworks is that the competencies are all compatible and that it is possible to be strong in all of them. Psychologically, there are grounds for challenging this assumption. More pragmatically, however, the advice might be to leave plenty of time to think through the use of tests in this context, and to realise that they seldom map on neatly to competencies – other assessment methods will be needed.

The role of the BPS in promoting higher standards of test use

The most ambitious step to improve test usage recently was taken by the British Psychological Society, with the full support of the CIPD, by introducing the assessment of competence in psychological testing. The first stage of this, the Level A statement of competence in occupational testing, dealt specifically with ability tests, while the next stage, the Level B competence scheme, dealt with the use of personality and interest measures. Together they represent a requirement for substantial breadth and depth of knowledge of underlying theory and principles to be certified as competent in personality testing. (Indeed, Level A is a prerequisite before even starting Level B.) Previously, it was sufficient to attend the relevant test supplier's courses, which understandably tended to be more narrowly focused on the particular personality measure in question. Although such courses are still obviously necessary, they do not in themselves provide an adequate basis for full Level B competence.

At the end of the day, however, all this effort to raise standards depends for its success on the desire of test-users to increase their competence and expertise. Those purveying tests of doubtful quality are only too quick to offer them without any questions asked. Indeed, they would probably prefer to be selling to customers who have not attained the Level B competence –

because anyone who has is more likely to identify unsound tests and to reject them. The number of HR staff who seek to achieve Level B competence will perhaps be a good yardstick by which to judge the extent to which there is a genuine desire within the profession to improve practice in the difficult area of personality assessment. At the time of writing 4,606 had obtained the Level B intermediate certificate, and 62 the Level B full certificate. The other, associated step is the publication by the BPS of Level A and Level B test reviews mentioned earlier in this chapter, available at its online Testing Centre.

Test publishers told us that they believed that standards of test use in the UK compared favourably with those in the rest of the world. However, we would ask if enough is being done. It seems to be rare for people to fail Level A and Level B training courses, although some publishers told us that that those who cannot reach the required standard are counselled before reaching the point of being assessed and failed. We found that the Psychological Testing Centre does not keep any information about the numbers who do not reach the required standard, the numbers who are asked to qualify again, or those with certificates who are subject to any kinds of complaint or discipline. Further, once the certificates are awarded, they remain valid for life – we know of no checks as to whether people are using and updating their skills, although we understand that continuing professional development (CPD) is being considered by the BPS steering committee on test standards. Certainly we have come across individuals who are operating as consultants on the basis of the short training courses designed to help them to use tests within a single organisation (see case study 9, page 6).

CONCLUDING COMMENTS

In the Preface to this Fourth Edition we said that we had four aims:

- to alert readers to the benefits of 'good' testing
- to warn of the disadvantages and dangers of 'bad' testing
- to give a 'balanced view' of the merits and disadvantages of testing, illustrating points by means of case studies and frequently asked questions
- to let readers decide whether to use tests (or continue testing) in the future.

We hope that readers will feel that we have achieved these aims and that they have a better understanding of what 'good' testing can achieve and how they can make sound decisions about testing in the future.

Keeping informed about future developments

Within the UK, the main source of information about aptitude and other tests comes from occupational psychologists and from their professional organisation, the British Psychological Society (for the address, see Appendix I). Readers are strongly advised to employ only chartered occupational psychologists, whose names and addresses appear in a register published by the BPS. It also publishes *Selection and Development Review*, a journal devoted to the critical review of assessment methods, other articles covering practical and political issues relating to assessment and counselling, up-to-date information on courses in testing to be held during the following two to three months, and reviews of recent academic articles of interest. The BPS also publishes an academic journal, *The Journal of Occupational and Organisational Psychology*, and runs conferences and other events for psychologists. Non-psychologists can attend conferences and other events by invitation. Some of these conferences and events cover the use of psychological tests and related methods such as assessment centres.

Readers from outside the UK and international organisations may find it helpful to keep in touch with the psychological societies, test publishers and leading consultants in the countries in which they are operating. Such information is available from the International Test Commission, whose objectives are to compare practices in the use of tests throughout the world.

This book has been published under the auspices of the Chartered Institute of Personnel and Development, which has more than 100,000 members in the United Kingdom. Articles on the use of tests are published in its fortnightly publication *People Management*. The CIPD also runs courses on the use of tests and other selection procedures, details of which are available from the Institute's Course and Conference Department. Further details about test publishers are available in the form of an information note from the CIPD's Information and Advisory Services Department. Because these details change from time to time they are not reproduced in full in this book, but details of the major suppliers of tests described in Chapter 3 have been given in Appendix I.

Appendix I
Test suppliers

ASE
The Chiswick Centre, 414 Chiswick High Road, London, W4 5TF
020 8996 8444
www.nfer-nelson.co.uk

The **Criterion Partnership**
Church Ward Court, 15 Western Road, Lewes, East Sussex, BN7 1RL
01273 480583

The **Morrisby Organisation**
83 High Street, Hemel Hempstead, Hertfordshire, HP1 3AH
01442 268645
www.morrisby.co.uk

OPP Oxford Psychologists Press Ltd
Lambourne House, 311–321 Banbury Road, Oxford, OX2 7JH
01865 510203
www.opp.co.uk

The **Psychological Corporation** Ltd
24–28 Oval Road, London, NWI 7DX
020 7267 4466
www.tpc-international.com

Psytech International Ltd
The Grange, Church Road, Pullox Hill, Bedfordshire, MK45 5HE
01525 20003
www.psytech.co.uk

SHL Saville and Holdsworth Ltd
The Pavilion, 1 Atwell Place, Thames Ditton, Surrey, KT7 0NE
0870 070 8000
www.shlgroup.com

The **Test Agency**
Burgner House, 4630 Kingsgate, Oxford Business Park South, Oxford, OX4 2SU
01865 714733
www.testagency.com

There are other test suppliers in the UK. The Chartered Institute of Personnel and Development keeps an up-to-date list of suppliers and copies can be sent to members on request.

Chartered Institute of Personnel and Development
Camp Road, London, SW19 4UX
020 8971 9000
Fax: 020 8263 3333

British Psychological Society
48 Princess Road East, Leicester, LE1 7DR
0116 254 9568

Appendix II

Assessing the worth of large correlations

In the early days of psychological testing, researchers and others tended to design tests to measure particular attributes and then went on to assess the worth of the test by correlating test scores against a performance criterion (eg scores on a test of mechanical aptitude against success as an apprentice). The correlations were carried out by hand and were slow and laborious to do.

Following on from this earlier work, there is still a widespread view among test-users that correlations provide a way of deciding whether or not to use tests in a particular situation. However, times have changed in four ways:

- First, many tests and questionnaires now produce a series of scores about each individual – one well-known personality questionnaire produces 32!

- Second, it is now more common to collect a number of measures covering different aspects of job performance: quantity and quality of output, performance on different kinds of task, and so on.

- Third, many studies relating test scores to performance at work and other behaviour are no longer designed to test specific predictions; instead, researchers conduct 'fishing trips' through a mass of data to see if any interesting correlations can be found.

- Fourth, the advent and widespread use of powerful small computers and statistical packages means that a mass of correlations can be carried out almost at the touch of a button.

Within the mass of correlations now being produced it is likely that some large and significant correlations will have occurred by chance. The widespread view that correlations can help to identify tests that may be of value has to change to meet these new circumstances.

In our view, test-users and others making decisions about tests should look for evidence of worth over and above the size of correlation. Four kinds of evidence that could be considered are:

- First, is there evidence that the correlation has come from a scientifically rigorous study that has aimed to test specific predictions (hypotheses) about the relationship between test scores and performance? Such an approach is of particular importance when assessing the values of scales on personality questionnaires, each of which can be regarded as a separate test from the point of view both of making predictions and of subsequent statistical analysis.

- Second, is there evidence that an appropriate level of statistical significance has been applied to check that the correlation has not occurred by chance? For example, if a specific prediction or hypothesis is being tested, it might be appropriate to set a 5 per cent level of significance (ie that results would occur by chance only 5 times in 100). However, if 'evidence' comes from a large matrix of correlations (say, more than 50) and no specific predictions have been made in advance, a 2 per cent or even 1 per cent level of significance would seem more appropriate.

- Third, can researchers or others offer some theoretical or practical explanations for any large correlations that have been found?

- Fourth, have similar findings been made in independent studies – or can such independent studies be arranged? Unfortunately, finding evidence in the scientific literature is easier said than done, since journals and other publications have little interest in validation studies, let alone those studies that are not 'positive' in the sense of breaking new ground.

Appendix III

Taking tests and receiving feedback

As a whole, this book has been written for managers. However, managers are sometimes asked about testing by colleagues, relatives or friends who may have little or no experience of testing and who may wonder if they can prepare for the experience in any way. This appendix has been written with such enquiries in mind.

The first part of this appendix deals with taking tests as part of a selection procedure; the next part deals briefly with obtaining 'feedback' from employers; and the remainder of the appendix deals with taking tests as part of counselling or guidance.

From the start it is important to be clear which kind of situation you are going to be facing since terms such as 'development centre' can cause confusion. Sometimes development centres are an opportunity to discuss your future with independent facilitators who are there to help you, and none of the information that you give the assessors will be passed on to your employer or to any other third party. However, other 'development centres' may in fact be part of a selection process, and you must then expect all the information that you reveal to be used in the decision-making process.

At the start of a well-designed selection process, you should be given clear information about the vacancy and about the kind of person that the employer is seeking to fill it. This will help you decide whether or not you should apply. Written applications (on applications forms or as CVs) are normally requested so that the most promising applicants can be selected on the basis of their applications and invited to attend the selection procedure. If you are invited to a well-designed selection procedure you should be sent a number of details in advance, including: (a) where the procedure is taking place, (b) when you should arrive, (c) who will be there to meet you, (d) the people who will assess you, (e) the selection techniques that will be used (eg the types of tests, the other procedures that will be involved, etc), (f) when a decision will be made, and (g) whether you will be reimbursed for travelling or other expenses.

The notes that follow deal only with preparation for testing.

TAKING TESTS AS PART OF A SELECTION PROCEDURE

To be successful at a selection procedure you must reach the required standard. If there are more applicants than vacancies (and this is nearly always the case), you must also show that you are one of the better candidates. Often there is only one vacancy, and if that is the case, you will have to show that you are the best candidate overall.

If the selection procedure involves reasoning or similar tests, you may be given a test description handout in advance of the procedure. The handout may tell you how the test will be presented to you (eg paper and pencil, or computer-based), how long it will last, and how you will be expected to make your replies (eg writing the answer, shading boxes on a form for computer scoring, or pressing keys on a keyboard). Most importantly, the handout may give examples of the kinds of question that you may be facing in the test itself.

If you have little or no experience of the test items shown as examples, you may wish to practise by referring to books which contain similar questions (and which provide answers too). These might be school or college textbooks dealing with a specific subject – eg how to calculate percentages, or you may choose to look at books on psychology which contain examples of questions used in reasoning tests. In deciding whether or not to prepare, consider the following points:

- Is there any information about whether the example items are representative of the rest of the test, or whether they merely illustrate some of the items in the test? For example, does a sample question involving percentages mean that all the questions will involve percentages, or does it mean that there will be a variety of mathematical calculations in the test itself including percentages, fractions, decimals, etc? Although the test should reflect the content of the work to be done if you are successful, it might be prudent to check this point with the person arranging the selection procedure.

- If the test items reflect abilities or skills that you have not used recently, and if there is opportunity to practise, it may be worth investing some time and effort in researching and practising the skills. On the other hand, if the test items reflect abilities and skills you have always found difficult, you may decide to withdraw on this occasion. If you really want to pass the test and to be offered that kind of work, it might be better to prepare for some time, perhaps even enrolling for relevant courses at a local college or elsewhere.

If the selection procedure involves personality questionnaires or similar techniques, it will not be appropriate to revise by going to the library and looking in books. The aim of such questionnaires is to build up a pattern of your interests and preferences, your likes and dislikes. Accordingly, your preparation might be in terms of

- reflecting on the things that you prefer to do, that you enjoy, etc, and contrasting these with situations that you prefer to avoid, dislike, etc

- reflecting too on your personal flexibility – to what extent are you willing to do work that doesn't interest you in order to take on a new job and to be successful at it?

- also reflecting on the extent to which your preferences and other behaviours really affect you – for example, most people are a little apprehensive before making a presentation: are you someone who is really nervous or just a little apprehensive too?

- finally, looking at the results of any previous assessments – do you feel (and did others feel) that the profile was a fair reflection of how you feel and how you are likely to come across to others? Might this influence how you answer the questions this time?

Personality questionnaires do not have right or wrong answers. What happens is that a number of questions are designed to measure a particular quality (eg self-confidence). A person who indicates high self-confidence on each of the individual questions will have a profile that indicates a high level of self-confidence overall.

There is a fine line between answering the questions in a way that is likely to give a true picture of your personality, preferences, etc, and answering the questions in a way that may increase your chances of getting a job. For example, someone lacking in self-confidence might be tempted to describe himself or herself as being confident in order to get a job. However, few employers rely solely on replies to personality questionnaires, so the deception may be found out with ease. Further, if the deception did work, there would then be the issue of whether a timid applicant could cope with the job demanding self-confidence in practice.

OBTAINING FEEDBACK FROM EMPLOYERS

Whether or not you are successful, it is worth asking for feedback about your performance not only on the tests but in the other parts of the assessment process. It will be helpful if you can clarify whether you met the standard for the job. If you met the standard but didn't get the job, it might be worth applying again in the future or seeking a similar job elsewhere. If you didn't meet the standard, it might be worth reflecting on whether you might be seen as a stronger applicant for a different kind of work (see below).

So far as your performance on the reasoning tests is concerned, try to clarify

- whether you reached the required standard overall
- whether, if you made errors, they were in response to a particular kind of question – eg did you get all the percentages wrong?

So far as your replies to personality and similar questionnaires are concerned, try to establish

- whether your profile was in line with the kind of profile generally sought for this kind of work
- whether a particular kind of profile was being sought in order to 'fit' with the rest of the team, and whether and in what ways your profile matched it.

In the light of this feedback you will have to decide (a) whether your responses to the questionnaire gave a fair picture of you, and (b) whether you feel that the implications drawn from your profile were fair to you. This may influence the way that you reply to future questionnaires or the way that you discuss the resulting profiles with potential employers.

Commercial pressures mean that few employers feel that they can afford to give detailed feedback to unsuccessful candidates, and some may fear debating outcomes in case it is the first sign of the decision being taken to apply to an employment tribunal. Even though you may have spent a day or more attending the selection procedure, employers tend to lose interest in unsuccessful applicants once selection decisions have been made. Accordingly, the way that you ask for feedback may be critical in terms of the response that you get – a telephone enquiry seeking information in a few areas may be more successful than a formal request seeking detailed written feedback.

TAKING TESTS AS PART OF COUNSELLING OR GUIDANCE

If your only experience of taking tests is as part of a selection procedure for a job, you may not experience the full benefit of testing. There are several reasons.

- The tests that you are asked to take are likely to be closely related to the specific vacancy. Accordingly, even if the employer is willing to give you feedback, it can only be in relation to the particular vacancy. There may be little indication of which kind of work you might do best or which kind of work might would best suit you.

- Few employers can offer a very wide range of jobs or have staff with the skills to offer career advice.

People therefore sometimes seek professional advice to check that they have identified the strongest of their abilities and to ensure that they have a good understanding of their motivation and preferences and of the way they come across to others. Advice can help target their job applications and/or construct personal development plans with a view to developing strengths and overcoming any shortcomings. Sometimes important dilemmas must be identified and resolved. For example, some people are bored by what they can do and set their minds on jobs for which they have little or no experience – they then become frustrated by the predictable rejections and/or the low starting salaries that they are offered because they lack experience.

Other parts of this book have drawn attention to the dangers of seeking advice about testing from people who have little or no training and no recognised qualifications. In our view, advice should be sought from chartered psychologists and others with suitable qualifications and experience. Sometimes this advice is available at little or no cost from careers services working for local authorities, university appointments services, etc.

Appendix IV

Specimen external assessment report

This is an example of a competency-based individual assessment (although only the competency headings are presented in this report) of a candidate for a top-level management post in the public sector. The format of the report and the competency headings are those chosen by the organisation concerned. They commission the assessments of those short-listed in advance of the interview panel, so that members of the latter can follow up on points raised during the interview (hence the Areas for probing section).

PSYCHOLOGIST'S REPORT

Interview 31 July 2001

Summary

Strengths

- Open-minded in listening to ideas from others and highly objective in evaluating his own contribution
- Approachable, amiable and strongly focused on a team approach
- Exceptional emotional stability and copes well with pressure

Areas for probing

- Basic shyness and a leadership style somewhat lacking in charisma; will he inspire the commitment of others and get his message across quickly enough?
- Though friendly and positive in his attitude to people, has he sufficient capacity to empathise with them and to be sensitive to their point of view – will he read them right?
- Does he think in strategic terms, or is he rather more task-focused?

Impact and influencing

Peter is somewhat shy, introverted and undemonstrative by nature, and gives a slightly low-key first impression. He takes some while to get to know well. Forming relationships is not something that comes naturally to him, so he has to work hard at it. He uses his interest in sport and other aspects of his life outside work to help establish more personal contact with people. Once past his initial reserve, colleagues and others will find that he is a genuine, honest and very amiable person who will win their confidence and trust. He is straightforward in the way he presents himself and in his use of words. He (rightly) does not see himself as being intellectually very high-powered, but he has developed his self-belief to the point where he has been able to stand up to some formidable opposition. He can assert himself effectively, but his style is essentially conciliatory rather than confrontational.

Leadership

He is a modest and open-minded individual who emphasises team effort – one of the lessons he feels he has learned is that his role is not to deliver personally, it is to facilitate others delivering. His subordinates will find him to be very approachable. He tends to downplay hierarchical differences and will try to consult directly with the sources of the information needed, whatever level they may be at in the organisation. His preference is very much for one-to-one contact, and he has little liking for large meetings. Where he has to put a team together, he will do so in a planned and systematic manner, building in some diversity. He will be more willing than most to listen to other people's ideas and more objective in his evaluation of them. He will readily put aside his own proposals when someone else comes up with better solutions – there may be times when he is almost too reasonable in this respect. He has the capacity to accept criticism of his own work in a constructive way and to learn from it. His leadership style may lack charisma, but it will slowly and quietly generate confidence, good communication and commitment.

Motivation and resilience

Compared to top managers as a group, Peter has an average level of energy and determination. His ambition and confidence have steadily grown, however. He feels he developed a good deal in his mid-30s and then began not only to feel that he could do a top-level job but actually started wanting to. He has been 'pleasantly surprised' that he has proved equal to each successive move upwards, which perhaps reflects his lack of intellectual arrogance. He is exceptionally emotionally stable, and will show a remarkably even temperament. Indeed, such is his own calmness, he may sometimes not be as sensitive as he should be in identifying signs of worry or stress in others. He will take setbacks in his stride and will cope effectively with pressure.

Managing change and decision-making

He is average for the top management group in terms of analytical reasoning, and he has a useful capacity for thinking imaginatively when faced with novel situations. His approach to problems may be more notable for its practical orientation than for its quality of strategic analysis. However, although there may be intellectually sharper members of the top team, Peter will use the ability he possesses to the maximum effectiveness. He will achieve a sound balance in steering a course between being cautious and taking risks, and will draw constructively on the experience and advice of others. He will display a good level of flexibility in responding to change, being able to adapt his approach quickly to meet new circumstances. His way of dealing with changes is such that he will usually carry his team with him.

Professor Clive Fletcher

References

Anastasi, A. (1998) *Psychological Testing* (6th edn). New York, Macmillan.

Anderson, N. and West, M. (1994) *Team Climate Inventory*. Windsor, ASE.

Anderson, N., Born, M. and Cunningham-Snell, N. (2001) 'Recruitment and selection; applicant perspectives and outcomes', in N. Anderson, D. Ones, H. Sinangil and C. Viswesvaran (eds) *International Handbook of Industrial, Work and Organizational Psychology*. Sage.

Ash, P. (1991) *The Construct of Employee Theft Proneness*. Park Ridge, IL, SRA/London House.

Audit Commission (1995) *Management Handbook: Paying the piper and calling the tune*. London, HMSO.

Baldry, C. and Fletcher, C. (1997) 'The integrity of integrity testing', *Selection and Development Review*, 13, 3–6.

Barrick, M. R. and Mount, M. K. (1991) 'The Big Five personality dimensions and job performance: a meta-analysis', *Personnel Psychology*, 44, 1–26.

Bartram, D. (1995) *Review of Personality Assessment Instruments (Level B) for use in Occupational Settings*. Leicester, BPS Books.

Bartram, D. (2001) 'Frames of mind', *People Management*, 14 June.

Bedford, T. and Feltham, R. T. (1986) *A Cost Benefit Analysis of the Extended Interview Method*. Home Office Unit at CSSB, Report No. 2.

Belbin, R. M. (2004) *Management Teams: Why they succeed or fail* (2nd edn). London, Heinemann.

Bentz, V. J. (1985) 'Research findings from personality assessment of executives', in H. G. Bernadin and D. A. Bownas (eds) *Personality Assessment in Organisations*. New York, Praeger.

Boyatzis, R. E. (1982) *The Competent Manager*. New York, John Wiley & Sons.

Camara, W. J. and Schneider, D. L. (1995) 'Questions of construct breadth and openness of research in integrity testing', *American Psychologist*, 50, 459–60.

Chan, K-Y., Drasgow, F. and Sawin, L. (1998) 'What is the shelf life of a test? The effect of time on the psychometrics of a cognitive ability test battery', *Journal of Applied Psychology*, 84, 4, 610–19.

Chartered Institute of Personnel and Development (1997) *The CIPD Guide on Psychological Testing*. London, CIPD.

Chartered Institute of Personnel and Development (2001) *Recruitment Survey Report*, May. London, CIPD.

Cooper, D., Robertson, I. T. and Tinline, G. (2003) *Recruitment and Selection: A framework for success*. Psychology@Work Series. London, Thomson.

Cronbach, L. J. (1984) *Essentials of Psychological Testing* (4th edn). New York, Harper & Row.

Cunningham, M. R., Wong, D. T. and Barbee, A. P. (1994) 'Self-presentation dynamics on overt integrity tests: experimental studies of the Reid Report', *Journal of Applied Psychology*, 79, 5, 643–58.

Czerny, A. (2004) 'Support for ethical testing', *People Management*, 11 March.

Dulewicz, S. V. (1989). 'Assessment centres as the route to competence', *Personnel Management*, November.

Dulewicz, S. V. (1991) 'Improving the effectiveness of assessment centres', *Personnel Management*, June.

Dulewicz, V. (1998) *Personal Competency Framework Manual*. Windsor, NFER-Nelson.

Dulewicz, V. (2004) 'Give full details . . . Online graduate recruitment: alienating candidates and selecting the wrong ones?', *People Management*, 26 February.

Fletcher, C. (1985) 'Feedback of psychometric test results: how great is the demand?', *Guidance and Assessment Review*, 6, 1/2 December.

Fletcher, C. (1991) 'Candidates' reactions to assessment centres and their outcomes: a longitudinal study', *Journal of Occupational Psychology*, 64, 117–27.

Fletcher, C. (1995) 'What means to assess integrity?', *People Management*, August, 30–31.

Fletcher, C. (1997) 'The impact of psychometric assessment: fostering positive candidate attitudes and reactions', *Selection and Development Review*, 13, 8–11.

Fletcher, C. (1998) 'Fraught process', *People Management*, 4, 13, 42–5.

Fletcher, C. and Williams, R. (1996) 'Performance management, job satisfaction and organisational commitment', *British Journal of Management*, 7, 169–79.

Gaugler, B., Rosenthal, D., Thornton, C. G. and Bentson, B. (1987) 'Meta-analysis of assessment centre validity', *Journal of Applied Psychology*, 72, 3.

Ghiselli, E. E. (1966) *The Validity of Occupational Aptitude Tests*. New York, Wiley.

Highhouse, S. (2003) 'Assessing the candidate as a whole: a historical and critical analysis of individual psychological assessment for personnel decision-making', *Personnel Psychology*, 55, 363–96.

Huffcutt, A. I. and Roth, P. L. (1998) 'Racial group differences in employment interview evaluations', *Journal of Applied Psychology*, 83, 2, 179–89.

Hunter, J. E. and Schmidt, F. L. (1982) 'The economic benefits of personnel selection using psychological ability tests', *Industrial Relations*.

Iles, P. A. and Robertson, I. T. (1995) 'The impact of personnel selection procedures on candidates', in N. Anderson and P. Herriot (eds) *Assessment and Selection in Organizations* (2nd update). London, John Wiley & Sons.

Johnson, C., Saville, P. and Fletcher, C. (1989) 'A test by any other name', *Personnel Management*, March, 47–51.

Kellett, D. and Toplis, J. (1989) 'Quality standards for the development and use of psychological tests', *Guidance and Assessment Review*, 5, 4, 4–8.

Klimoski, R. J. and Rafaeli, A. (1983) 'Inferring personal qualities through handwriting analyis', *Journal of Occupational Psychology*, 56, 191–202.

Kline, P. (1998) *A Handbook of Test Construction*. London, Methuen.

Lewis, C. (1985) *Employee Selection* (Personnel Management Series). London, Hutchinson.

Lounsbury, J. W., Bobrow, W. and Jensen, J. B. (1989) 'Attitudes to employment testing: scale development, correlates and "known group" validation', *Professional Psychology: Research and Practice*, 20, 340–9.

McHenry, R. (2001) 'Frames of mind', *People Management*, 14 June.

Michigan Employability Survey (1989) in *The Use of Integrity Tests for Pre-Employment Screening* (1990). Washington, DC, US Congress, Office of Technology Assessment.

Miller, K. M. (ed.) (1975) *Psychological Testing in Personnel Assessment*. Essex, Gower Press.

Moses, J. L. (1985) 'Using clinical methods in a high level management assessment center', in H. G. Bernadin and D. S. Bownas (eds) *Personality Assessment in Organisations*. New York, Praeger.

Murphy, K. R. and Lee, S. L. (1994) 'Personality variables related to integrity test scores: the role of conscientiousness', *Journal of Business and Psychology*, 8, 4, 413–24.

Newell, S. (1995) *The Healthy Organization* (Essential Business Psychology Series). London, Routledge.

Ones, D. S., Schmidt, F. L., Viswesvaran, C. and Lykken, D. T. (1996) 'Controversies over integrity testing: two viewpoints', *Journal of Business and Psychology*, 10, 4, 487–501.

People Management (2001a) Editorial, 14 June.

People Management (2001b) News section, 9 August.

Pickard, J. (1996) 'The wrong turns to avoid with tests', *People Management,* 9 August, 20–5.

Ployhart, R. E. and Ryan, A. M. (1998) 'Applicants' reactions to the fairness of selection procedures: the effects of positive rule violation and time of measurement', *Journal of Applied Psychology*, 83, 3–16.

Reilly, R. R. and Chao, G. T. (1982) 'Validity and fairness of some alternative employee selection procedures', *Personnel Psychology*, 35, 1–62.

Robertson, I. T. and Makin, P. J. (1986) 'Management selection in Britain: a survey and critique', *Journal of Occupational Psychology*, 59, 1, 45–58.

Rodger, A. (1953) *The Seven Point Plan*. Windsor, NFER-Nelson.

Roth, P. L., Bobko, P. and Mabon, H. (2000) 'Utility analysis: a review and analysis at the turn of the century', in N. Anderson, D. Ones, H. Sinangil and C. Viswesvaran (eds) *International Handbook of Industrial, Work and Organizational Psychology*. Sage.

Rynes, S. L. (1993) 'Who's selecting whom? Effects of selection practices on applicant attitudes and behavior', in N. Schmitt, W. Borman and Associates (eds) *Personnel Selection in Organizations*. San Francisco, Jossey-Bass.

Rynes, S. L and Connerly M. L. (1993) 'Applicant reactions to alternative selection procedures', *Journal of Business and Psychology*, 7, 261–77.

Rynes, S. L., Heneman, H. G. and Schwab, D. P. (1980) 'Individual reactions to organizational recruiting: a review', *Personnel Psychology*, 33, 529–42.

Sackett, P. R. and Harris, M. M. (1984) 'Honesty testing for personnel selection: a review and critique', *Personnel Psychology*, 37, 221–45.

Schmidt, F. L. and Hunter, J. E. (1979) 'The impact of valid selection procedures on workforce productivity', *Journal of Applied Psychology*, 64, 609–26.

Schmidt, F. L and Hunter J. E. (1998) 'The validity and utility of selection methods in personnel psychology: practical and theoretical implications of 85 years of research findings', *Psychological Bulletin*, 124, 2, September, 262–74.

Schwartz, Steven (Chairman) (2004) 'Fair admissions to higher education: Draft recommendations for consultation'. www.admissions-review.org.uk

Silvester, J. and Brown, A. (1993) 'Graduate recruitment: testing the impact', *Selection and Development Review*, 9, 1, 1–3.

Smith, M. (1986) 'Selection: where are the best prophets?', *Personnel Management*, December, 63.

Society for Industrial and Organisational Psychology (1987) *Principles for the validation and use of Personnel Selection Procedures*. Maryland, the University of Maryland.

Stagner, R (1958) 'The gullibility of personnel managers', *Personnel Psychology*, 11, 347–52.

Toplis, J. W. (1970) 'Studying people at work', *Journal of Occupational Psychology*, 44, 95–114.

Toplis, J. W. and Stewart, B. (1983) 'Group selection methods', in B. Ungerson (ed.) *Recruitment Handbook* (3rd edn). Hampshire, Gower Press.

Weisner, W. H. and Cronshaw, S. F. (1988) 'A meta-analytic investigation of the impact of interview format and degree of structure on the validity of the employment interview', *Journal of Occupational Psychology*, 61, 275–90.

Wolff, C. J. de (1989) 'The changing role of psychologists in selection', in P. Herriot (ed.) *Assessment and Selection in Organisations*. Chichester, Wiley.

Woodruffe, C. (2000) *Development and Assessment Centres*. London, CIPD.

Index